Human–Computer Interaction Series

SpringerBriefs in Human-Computer Interaction

SpringerBriefs in Human-Computer Interaction presents concise research within the fast growing, multidisciplinary field of Human-Computer Interaction (HCI). Designed to complement Springer's prestigious *Human-Computer Interaction Series*, this Briefs series provides researchers with a forum to publish cutting-edge scientific material relating to any emerging HCI research that is not yet mature enough for a volume in the *Human-Computer Interaction Series,* but which has evolved beyond the level of a journal or workshop paper.

SpringerBriefs in Human-Computer Interaction are shorter works of 50-125 pages in length, allowing researchers to present focused case studies, summaries and introductions to state-of-the-art research. They are subject to the same rigorous reviewing processes applied to the *Human-Computer Interaction Series* but offer exceptionally fast publication.

Topics covered may include but are not restricted to:

- User Experience and User Interaction Design
- Pervasive and Ubiquitous Computing
- Computer Supported Cooperative Work and Learning (CSCW/CSCL)
- Cultural Computing
- Computational Cognition
- Augmented and Virtual Reality
- End-User Development
- Multimodal Interfaces
- Interactive Surfaces and Devices
- Intelligent Environment Wearable Technology

SpringerBriefs are published as part of Springer's eBook collection, with millions of users worldwide and are available for individual print and electronic purchase. Briefs are characterized by fast, global electronic distribution, standard publishing contracts, easy-to-use manuscript preparation and formatting guidelines and have expedited production schedules to help aid researchers disseminate their research as quickly and efficiently as possible.

Fred D. Davis • Andrina Granić

The Technology Acceptance Model

30 Years of TAM

 Springer

Fred D. Davis
Rawls College of Business
Texas Tech University
Lubbock, TX, USA

Andrina Granić
Faculty of Science
University of Split
Split, Croatia

The order of authorship was determined alphabetically.

ISSN 1571-5035   ISSN 2524-4477   (electronic)
Human–Computer Interaction Series
ISSN 2520-1670   ISSN 2520-1689   (electronic)
SpringerBriefs in Human-Computer Interaction
ISBN 978-3-030-45273-5   ISBN 978-3-030-45274-2   (eBook)
https://doi.org/10.1007/978-3-030-45274-2

This Springer imprint is published by the registered company Springer Nature Switzerland AG
The registered company address is: Gewerbestrasse 11, 6330 Cham, Switzerland

Paper in this product is recyclable.

To my daughters, Ana and Dora,
your love lights up my life. (Andrina)

Contents

List of Figures

List of Tables

Chapter 1
Introduction: "Once Upon a TAM"

Abstract The chapter delves into Fred's retrospective account of developing the Technology Acceptance Model (TAM), shedding light on the model's conceptualization process. In the 1980s, the prevalent challenge of high rejection rates for new systems led to the belief that predicting user acceptance might be an unsolvable problem. TAM challenged this notion, asserting that consistent prediction, explanation and improvement of user acceptance are indeed achievable. The model's success was attributed to advancements in theory and measurement. To enhance contemporary attitude theory, the centralization of attitude toward using a target system was crucial. Attitude, causally connected to intention and behaviour, played a key role in predicting usage. However, for the model to explain why individuals develop positive or negative attitudes toward system use, identifying pertinent beliefs or perceptions was necessary. TAM identified two key overlooked drivers of user acceptance – perceived usefulness and perceived ease of use. These beliefs act as determinants of attitude, creating links in the causal chain connecting system design features to user acceptance. They form the core of the original model and remain at its heart. The resulting TAM model proved remarkably effective, initiating extensive subsequent research supporting its predictive and explanatory capabilities. TAM stands as the leading model for predicting and explaining user acceptance.

Keywords User acceptance crystal ball · Technology Acceptance Model · TAM · Origins · Conceptualization · Development · Specification · Leading model

1.1 Opening Remarks

Wouldn't it be great if we had a crystal ball that could predict user acceptance of new information systems? This question motivated Fred Davis's 1986 Massachusetts Institute of Technology (MIT) Ph.D. dissertation "A Technology Acceptance Model for Empirically Testing New End-User Information Systems: Theory and Results" (Davis, 1986). Such a crystal ball could cut losses from doomed systems, guide changes needed to rescue trouble systems under development and prioritize resource

© The Author(s), under exclusive license to Springer Nature
Switzerland AG 2024
F. D. Davis, A. Granić, *The Technology Acceptance Model*, Human–Computer
Interaction Series, https://doi.org/10.1007/978-3-030-45274-2_1

allocation toward the most promising system concepts. It wouldn't need to be perfect to have value. Predicting better than chance could have benefits. For example, if the crystal ball could provide reliable directional advice about which of two system ideas has a better chance of success that would be helpful. In short, a user acceptance crystal ball could help cut the incidence of new systems failing to become embraced by target users.

The notion of trying to create a "user acceptance crystal ball" must have seemed foolhardy to many information systems practitioners and academics in the 1970s and 1980s. The high rejection rate for new systems was a lamentable fact of life. It was widely believed that predicting user acceptance was a problem that was not only unsolved, but might even be unsolvable. Numerous published articles had failed to identify predictors and create models to reliably predict successful system implementation. Many believed that user acceptance is inherently unpredictable, possibly driven by irrational factors such as political dynamics or general resistance to change.

The Technology Acceptance Model (TAM) introduced in Davis's dissertation (Davis, 1986) and two 1989 journal articles (Davis, 1989; Davis et al., 1989) challenged this received wisdom by proposing that it actually is possible to consistently predict, explain, and improve user acceptance. TAM's success was largely due to improved theory and improved measurement. Importantly, TAM (see Fig. 1.1) identified two key overlooked drivers of user acceptance: perceived usefulness and perceived ease of use. These are really the core of the original model and remain the core of TAM. The identification, development and measurement of these two constructs followed solid theoretical and psychometric principles. The resulting TAM model was surprisingly effective and triggered substantial follow-on research supporting its predictive and explanatory power. TAM remains the leading model for predicting and explaining user acceptance.

This book discusses the origins, emergence and evolution of TAM and should be of interest to system developers, project managers, user experience specialists, researchers, senior managers, teachers and policymakers. The rest of the chapter provides Fred's retrospective account of the origins of TAM.

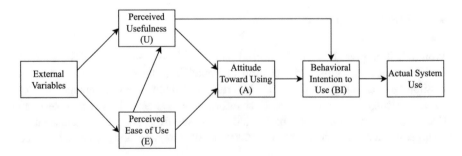

Fig. 1.1 Technology Acceptance Model, TAM. (Davis et al., 1989)

1.2   TAM Goals: Predict, Explain and Improve User Acceptance

A key goal underlying TAM was that it should be a practical tool that could be used by practitioners for "user acceptance testing" of new information systems early in their development. User reactions to demonstrations of prototypes captured by TAM should provide valuable information about the likely success of the eventual completed system. TAM's questionnaire instruments needed to be simple and effi-cient to administer in practice, but also valid for predicting the likely future accep-tance of the system. TAM needed to have the correct variables, and the variables needed to have valid and reliable measurements. The variables needed to link the design characteristics of the system, i.e. its functional and interface characteristics, to the eventual use/non-use behaviour.

Major goals for TAM were (1) identifying the important core determinants of user acceptance – perceived usefulness and perceived ease of use – and (2) develop-ing valid and reliable measures for perceived usefulness and perceived ease of use. The dissertation demonstrated that the validated measures of perceived usefulness and ease of use predict user acceptance, and they explain how objective differences between systems influence user acceptance. Perceived usefulness is the primary determinant of user acceptance, and perceived ease of use is a powerful secondary determinant that influences user acceptance both directly and indirectly through its influence on perceived usefulness. The primacy of perceived usefulness over ease of use is intuitive. Users will tolerate some difficulty of using a system if it provides critical functionality that enhances its usefulness. However, no amount of ease of use can compensate for a system that does not provide any useful benefits.

Importantly, the dissertation showed that perceived usefulness is stable and pre-dictive of user acceptance even when it is based on a non-interactive demonstration of a new system, with no hands-on interaction with the system. This stability, along with the relative importance of perceived usefulness over ease of use, creates oppor-tunities to push user acceptance testing earlier in the system development process, even before a working prototype is available, and still captures perceptions that are linked to and predictive of later user acceptance. In other words, potential users were able to form realistic and stable perceptions of usefulness without hands-on usage experience with the system, which did not change later based on hands-on experience. This stability of perceived usefulness between the non-interactive video demo and the hands-on introduction was not true of perceived ease of use. Ease of use perceptions shifted significantly after hands-on experience compared to what they were based on the video demo. This fits with the intuition that forming realistic ease of use perceptions requires hands-on experience to judge how easy or hard the system actually is to use. It may be somewhat counterintuitive that stable usefulness perceptions could be made without such hands-on experience, but it makes sense if usefulness perceptions are based much more on an assessment of what the system can do, and how that functionality matches a user's needs, than on how to use the system.

Overall, TAM is simple, powerful, practical, theory-based and validated. The core model is based on perceived usefulness and perceived ease of use, which are linked to and can be influenced by the choice of system design characteristics, i.e. functional and interface features. Perceived usefulness and perceived ease of use influence attitudes and intentions, which influence and predict user acceptance. TAM is thus able to *predict* user acceptance, *explain* the reasons for acceptance or rejection based on perceived usefulness and perceived ease of use and provide guidance to *improve* user acceptance by altering system design characteristics or other managerially controllable interventions that increase perceived usefulness or perceived ease of use. Over the more than three decades since TAM's introduction, there have been numerous extensions with additional variables. However, perceived usefulness and perceived ease of use remain the basic beliefs of the core TAM model.

1.3   Retrospective Account on the Origins of TAM

1.3.1   Backstory Late 1970s

Once upon a time in the late 1970s, I was getting my B.S. in Industrial Engineering at Wayne State University in Detroit. Coursework impressed me with a range of analytical tools spanning optimization, simulation and statistical analysis and the growing power of computer technology to drive these tools for solving real-world problems. Human Factors Engineering and Ergonomics classes cultivated interest and expertise in human-machine systems and user interface design. I took enough Computer Science courses to earn a minor, and I saw great opportunities to fuse analytics, computing and user insights.

Industrial Engineering courses warned about the high failure rate for real-world Operations Research/Management Science initiatives. Too often applications of analytical tools to industry problems, and their software implementations, were not embraced and used by clients. Those challenges were evident when I participated in several faculty-supervised field projects. There was a recognized need for better principles to reduce the failure rate and improve system implementation (e.g. Bostrom & Heinen, 1977).

I was employed while a student by a healthcare financial consulting firm owned by two Industrial Engineering professors. I designed and built several information systems to tackle budget development, financial modelling and reporting. I used System Development Life Cycle (SDLC) methodologies that were gaining popularity in computer science and data processing at the time, including the sequential waterfall approach, and experienced some of their strengths and limitations. I experienced the challenges of translating client needs into effective high-value functionality. Requirements statements were an imperfect guide for crafting specific functionality attuned to the nuances and complexities of planning and decision-making tasks. It was surprising how difficult it was, and how much code it took, to build user interfaces that are intuitive, efficient, flexible and reliable. I was learning first-hand how hard it is to build successful systems.

Around my third year, I faced the issue of what I wanted to do after graduation. I recognized the exploding capability of computer technology and its promise for harnessing powerful analytics and data management. I also recognized user acceptance as a critical link in the chain connecting technical innovations with value-added solutions to important business and societal problems. User acceptance was a pivotal issue, and more knowledge was needed about how to design new systems to achieve user acceptance and avoid costly implementation failure. Occasionally, I would take a study break by having a coffee and walking over to the nearby Detroit Institute of Arts. My favourite spot was the room surrounded by Diego River's inspirational "Detroit Industry" frescoes depicting the power of technology for driving industry. I became highly committed to work on overcoming the challenges of harnessing the power of information technology.

I saw a poster on our department bulletin board inviting applicants to study "Decision Support Systems" in the Ph.D. program at MIT's Sloan School of Management. It showed a diagram of a decision support system connecting a manager to his or her environment via data, information and decisions. The DSS included a model bank, data bank, statistical methods and an interface display. I thought "aha" – this diagram resonated with my vision of harnessing computing technology and analytic tools. With faculty encouragement, I applied to the MIT PhD program and got accepted. I finished my Industrial Engineering degree and started the MIT PhD program in Management Information Systems (MIS) in 1980. Off I went on my journey toward developing TAM.

1.3.2   Starting the MIT PhD Program 1980

It was thrilling to join the atmosphere of IT innovation surrounding MIT and Boston/Cambridge in 1980, with dozens of computer hardware and software companies all around. Venture capital was fuelling a seemingly endless parade of new tech start-ups. The early 1980s was a period of rapid transformation toward end-user access to computer technology. For example, in 1980 the MIT secretaries were using IBM Selectric typewriters, and few faculties had even dumb terminals in their offices. Office automation soon appeared in secretarial areas and terminals were showing up in faculty offices.

My coursework included optimization, statistics, and programming. I took many doctoral courses on behavioural theory and research methodology, including psychometrics, which is concerned with the development and validation of high-quality questionnaire measurement instruments. In doctoral seminars and my own independent study, I explored diverse behavioural theory bases that might be relevant for a dissertation on user acceptance, including attitude theory, work motivation, self-efficacy theory, behavioural decision theory, diffusion of innovations and so on. I took a graduate seminar with legendary Harvard motivation theorist David McClelland.

During my first 3 years, I participated in several faculty-led research projects with companies.

Meanwhile, the IBM PC was introduced in August 1981, and by 1982 PCs were standard in faculty offices. Lotus Development Corporation (Lotus 1-2-3 spreadsheets and Notes groupware) was founded in 1982, located adjacent to the Kendall Square location of MIT's Sloan School. The Macintosh was launched in January 1984 and was also showing up. In 1984, my own PhD student desk went from having no computer terminal at all to having a Xerox Star workstation (forerunner of the Macintosh interface with mouse, icons, windows and desktop metaphor). I wrote my dissertation using that Xerox Star.

Big changes were in the air. "User-centred design" practices emerged with their focus on early user testing of prototypes and highly iterative development (e.g. Gould & Lewis, 1985). With all the transformative change, it was a very fortunate time and place to do research on user acceptance.

1.3.3   What Problem Are We Solving Here? MIS Implementation Research

In my first year at MIT, I took Peter Keen's Decision Support Systems class, where we learned the state-of-the-art research on the information systems "implementation problem" concerning user rejection of new systems.

In the 1970s and 1980s, the problem of failed user acceptance for new systems was widespread. Keen and Scott Morton (1978, p. 189) reported "innumerable instances of models and systems being built but never used." This "implementation problem" was considered "the soft underbelly of information system development" (Keen & Scott Morton, 1978, p. 211). No general principles existed for predicting or explaining user acceptance, and it was widely agreed that "implementation will never be easy" (Keen & Scott Morton, 1978, p. 210).

Research showed that "...managers now clearly see that the implementation rate for computer projects has always been low" (Keen & Scott Morton, 1978, p. 189). Concerning reasons why projects fail at the time of implementation, Keen and Scott Morton (1978, p. 195) elaborate:

> ...many recent researchers argue that there are *no* general principles...it has become clear that there are no absolute factors that 'explain' implementation. For example, Ginzberg (1975) dissects 14 factor studies, all of which are extensive, well-researched, and, in their way, insightful. Each tries to answer the deceptively simple question: What are the factors that enhance the likelihood that an implementation effort will be successful?

The 14 papers identified 140 distinct factors purportedly relevant for successful IS implementation. However, Keen and Scott Morton (1978) observed inconsistencies and a lack of consensus across studies (p. 199). They observed that implementation "is a complex process and very few rules can be confidently applied." They guardedly summarized the literature (p. 196):

At best, we can conclude that the factors below are the only ones that have been plausibly
shown in a range of studies and settings to have substantial impact on the likelihood of success: i) top management support, ii) a clear felt need by the client, iii) an immediate, visible
problem to work on, iv) early commitment by the user and conscious staff involvement, and
v) a well-institutionalized OR/MS or MIS group.

Keen and Scott Morton's (1978) pessimistic outlook for predicting and explaining
system utilization was echoed by Swanson (1988) a decade later. Swanson defined
system implementation problems as "problems in bridging the gap between the
design of a system and its utilization" (p. 2). Swanson (1988) identified nine implementation factors that he likened to pieces of a jigsaw puzzle:

...success in information system implementation is a matter of establishing a fit among a
number of important factors, among which are user involvement, management commitment, value basis, mutual understanding, design quality, performance level, project management, resource adequacy, and situational stability. ... The solution to an implementation
puzzle is substantially more difficult than has thus far been portrayed. This may be under-
stood by introducing two implementation complexities not present in the traditional puzzle.
First, the shape of each piece is only partially observable. Second, the shape of each puzzle
piece is transformable to a limited degree.

Swanson (1988) identified between five and nine subfactors for each of the nine
factors, resulting in a collection of 55 subfactors. For example, the factor "project
management" includes the subfactors "lack of training package", "use of pilot" and
"poor timing in terms of deadlines". The indeterminacy regarding how to assess the
fit among the nine factors becomes exacerbated when expanding them into 55 constituent subfactors. Swanson (1988, p. 11) summarizes the situation: "the solution
to an implementation puzzle is indeed elusive!"

Overall, in the 1980s, the problem of user acceptance was widely recognized by
MIS Implementation research, even though solutions had not been established.
Research attempting to predict and explain user acceptance of new information systems was mixed and inconclusive. Different studies were inconsistent, with some
finding certain factors to be predictive, but other studies failing to confirm those
factors. I attributed this lack of progress to the diversity of belief and attitude measures being used without adequate theoretical or psychometric justification. I
believed that if I identified and defined the correct determinants of user acceptance
based on sound theoretical foundations, and then developed valid and reliable measures of them, we could make progress toward more consistent prediction and
explanation of user acceptance.

1.3.4   The Dissertation

The MIT faculty were sceptical when I said I wanted to tackle the problem of user
acceptance. They challenged me: "if so many smart people have failed, what makes
you think you can do it?" My response was "we need to use better theory and better
measurement". First, the MIS Implementation models published so far had not

taken advantage of some recent developments in several behavioural theories, which could provide guidance for identifying the most relevant predictive and explanatory constructs. Second, there was a growing awareness of the importance of using psychometrically valid and reliable measures of self-report constructs.

Even if a relevant construct is being theorized, if the measure of it lacks construct validity, i.e., it does not measure the intended construct, the measure may fail to demonstrate the true relationship of the construct to usage behaviour. Even if the measure is tapping into the intended relevant construct, if it is not reliable, random error could obscure its true relationship to usage behaviour. The psychometric approach calls for the use of multi-item scales to overcome inherent unreliability of individual items, allowing random measurement errors of individual questions to cancel out. Psychometrics defines principles to carefully design, select, pre-test and prioritize the multiple items used to assure they are valid and reliable. Overall, better theory and better measurement were the differentiators I was counting on to enable my dissertation to solve the problem of predicting user acceptance.

In formulating a dissertation strategy, I was influenced by a recent conference paper by Peter Keen (1980) in which he argued that the new MIS field should emulate practices of more established scientific disciplines to advance toward maturity. First, rather than trying to develop our own indigenous theories from scratch, we should draw upon knowledge that has been accumulating for decades in reference disciplines like economics, psychology, sociology, computer science etc. Second, we should seek to build more on the accumulated prior research published in our own journals to establish and build a cumulative tradition. I took both ideas to heart and they served me well.

1.4   TAM Theory Development Process

Over the years, many people have asked me how I came up with the TAM model. Theory development is a largely tacit and heuristic process, iterative and hard to explain. A few years ago, I made a presentation at Texas Tech University covering the origin and evolution of TAM. Management Professor Bill Gardner said my development of TAM was similar to the general process of developing Management theories documented by Smith and Hitt (2005). Based on interviews with the developers of 24 prominent Management theories, Smith and Hitt (2005) identified four distinct stages: tension, search, elaboration and proclamation:

- *Tension* involves contradictions, like those between existing theories and the researcher's observations.
- *Search* is driven by the resulting dissonance and commonly involves listening to and observing people in the workplace to discover and explore the phenomenon and develop a framework.

- *Elaboration* is often a seemingly endless iterative process of making sense out of observations, inductively consolidating and expanding ideas, connecting them to previous work and drawing pictures and diagrams.
- *Proclamation* involves formalizing the resulting model or theory and presenting it to the scientific community.

These common stages were generally linear, but in some cases overlapped, and/or there was movement back and forth among the stages. The process commonly entailed a combination of observing and talking to people in the workplace, reading and organizing published empirical studies and theories from sister disciplines and discussing with colleagues. Overall, the process of theory development involves synthesizing, reorganizing, shuffling and filtering existing ideas and empirical observations. The process is often tacit, with intuitive judgment calls and leaps of logic. Some authors reported progress unfolding gradually and others reported a sudden flash of insight.

Smith and Hitt's (2005) general description of theory development is helpful for describing my experience in developing TAM. I experienced confusion, foraging and gradual refinement, resulting in slightly different versions of the "original" TAM model as discussed below. I also had a distinct "aha moment" when things came together and crystallized for me during a short helicopter ride as described below.

1.4.1   Tension

The tension stimulating TAM theory development came from multiple sources. First, the premise of TAM goes against the received wisdom at the time among academics and practitioners that "everyone knows it can't be done". Predicting and explaining successful implementation was hit or miss. Findings were mixed and inconclusive. The main consistent research finding was that there are no consistent findings! When I would tell IS managers that for my dissertation "I want to predict in advance whether a new system would be accepted by the intended users", they would respond "ha ha, you and everybody else!". Some would ask "how do you propose to do that?" and I would explain "show users a demo or prototype mock-up, capture their reactions with a questionnaire, and use that to predict their future willingness to adopt the finished system". To this they might comment "that has been tried and it usually doesn't work because users don't know what they want and keep changing their minds". The voices of experience were seriously cautioning me about my chances for success.

The second tension surrounds the concept of "usability", which is typically defined as "extent to which a system, product or service can be used by specified users to achieve specified goals with effectiveness, efficiency and satisfaction in a specified context of use" (ISO 9241). Usability is widely considered a paramount criterion for a successful system, and I agree it captures critical elements of system success. However, it turns out to be incomplete, failing to fully capture whether or not users will be motivated to adopt and use the system. The "specified goals" are often not the actual goals of the users. Specified goals are usually tied to functionality defined in a project's statement of requirements, and a key reason for system failure is incorrect requirements. Just because the system *can* be used does not mean it *will* be used. TAM asserts that perceived usefulness is the primary determinant of user acceptance, and the goals a system is capable of achieving need to be important to the user for the system to be useful.

The usability concept does not fully capture the concept of perceived usefulness. Usefulness tends to be a "blind spot" in the usability lens. Many usability specialists argue that the "satisfaction" element covers perceived usefulness, and I partially agree. Systems are perceived to be useful as they satisfy a user's needs. Therefore, many assume that usability is a comprehensive umbrella that captures the key elements relevant to user acceptance. In practice, the term usability tends to confuse or equate usefulness and ease of use, which TAM argues are definitely distinct. Often usability gets interpreted to mean ease of use, and usefulness gets overlooked, neglected, discounted or forgotten.

The third tension relates to various pressures to schedule user testing late in the development process. System development life cycle methodologies typically schedule usability testing near the end of the project, after all other development and testing and before final sign off on the delivered system by the client, sponsor or customer. Textbook usability testing involves verifying that the system can carry out predefined test cases established earlier in the project as representative of the requirements. Usability testing confirms that the system can perform the intended functionality and that the user interface was easy enough to use. Typical test metrics include the success rate of completing test tasks, accuracy, errors and task completion time and often included a subjective assessment of "usability". It is not uncommon for new systems to pass user testing and then fail to achieve actual workplace acceptance by users. TAM advocates moving user testing earlier to detect and correct user acceptance issues before the end of the project, at which time it may be nearly impossible to remedy the underlying problems.

Human-Computer Interaction (HCI) specialists who advocate user-centred design recommend moving user testing earlier rather than waiting until the end. They recognize the value of getting early user feedback based on working prototypes and iteratively refining the evolving system design. A key idea behind TAM is that it should be possible to test system design ideas with users before there is even a working prototype. Some HCI specialists insist that user testing needs to be based on a working prototype to capture realistic user assessments. I agree that hands-on interaction with a representative working system is important for capturing realistic and meaningful ease of use perceptions. However, an important principle underlying TAM is that realistic and stable perceptions of usefulness do not require hands-on experience and can therefore be assessed earlier in the development process, before even a working prototype is available. The dissertation specifically shows that usefulness perceptions based on non-interactive video mock-ups of a system are highly correlated with later hands-on-based perceptions from the same participants. The ability to measure usefulness earlier than ease of use, coupled with the fact that usefulness is more important than ease of use, allows TAM to achieve the purpose of a user acceptance crystal ball, foretelling the user acceptance of a system before it even exists.

The way I described the three tensions suggests that I already knew about perceived usefulness from the outset. I admit I had a hunch that perceived usefulness was important and overlooked, but it still remained to be demonstrated. The hunch was based on my professional and academic field research experiences. I had seen many failed systems and recognized that they were missing something. Where are the benefits to the users? This hunch was reinforced by field research projects during my first couple of years in the PhD program. I participated in several sponsored research projects being done by MIT's Centre for Information Systems Research under director Professor Jack Rockart. These projects ranged from needs assessment studies to impact studies and involved interviewing users about their jobs, technology needs and experiences. I was forming a mental model of user acceptance based on what I used to refer to as "benefits". Across different types of technologies including teleconferencing, executive information systems, engineering workstations in R&D, collaborative groupware etc. I formed the idea that user unwillingness to adopt and use the technology was due to lack of benefits. Later I changed to the term "perceived usefulness" and defined it more specifically as perceptions of whether using the system would enhance one's job performance.

According to Smith and Hitt's (2005) interviews, theory development tensions typically arose from contradictions between the scholar's personal viewpoint and (a) the assumptions of existing theories and/or (b) observed business practices. For me it was both. My personal viewpoint based on extensive observation and discussion of real systems in the workplace was that perceived usefulness is essential to user acceptance, but the research models did not fully identify it, and system development practices did not fully recognize it.

All three of the tensions mentioned are connected to overlooking the concept of perceived usefulness: (1) a main reason why previous research and practice was unable to predict user acceptance is that they were not identifying the concept of perceived usefulness and measuring it reliably, (2) usability is a compelling but ultimately incomplete concept that has a critical blind spot concerning perceived usefulness and (3) pressures to delay user testing until near the end of the project, or at least until a working prototype is available, overlooks two key characteristics of perceived usefulness: it is more important than ease of use, and it can be realistically measured earlier.

1.4.2   Attitude Theory and the Theory of Reasoned Action

Because most of the factor studies in the MIS Implementation stream were questionnaire-based field studies that included various attitude and perception measures, it made sense to look into attitude theory from social psychology as a reference discipline. It was discouraging at first to learn that decades of research on the attitude-behaviour relationship had produced equivocal results; it was doubtful that attitudes could reliably predict behaviour. A promising recent development came from Ajzen and Fishbein (1977) showing that the strength of the attitude-behaviour relationship depended on how the attitude was defined and measured. Specifically, attitudes toward the object (A_o) of the behaviour (person, event etc.) are less likely to be correlated with specific behaviours toward that object. Instead, attitudes toward the specific behaviour (A_b) regarding the object are more likely to be correlated with the behaviour.

This idea of attitude-behaviour correspondence in specificity was a key building block of Fishbein and Ajzen's (1975) *Theory of Reasoned Action* (TRA) which differentiated between beliefs, attitudes, intentions and behaviours and specified how these constructs form a causal chain. TRA was a breakthrough in attitude research because it can consistently predict and explain a wide range of volitional behaviours. I had the good fortune of being invited to collaborate with Marketing professor Paul Warshaw on a series of three co-authored articles that we published in psychology journals. This collaboration provided me needed expertise to confidently draw upon attitude theory and specifically TRA as a reference discipline foundation for my dissertation.

To build on contemporary attitude theory, and specifically the Theory of Reasoned Action, it seemed essential to include "attitude toward the behaviour of using the target system" (A_b) as a central construct. A_b and its forward causal linkage to intention and behaviour, provided the part of the model needed for predicting usage. However, for the model to explain why people held a positive or negative A_b toward using the system, it was necessary to identify the salient beliefs or perceptions that underlie the formation of A_b. This can be seen as the process of moving upstream in the causal chain to find the belief-based antecedents of A_b. Identifying and measuring these antecedent beliefs is important not only for explaining or diagnosing why individuals hold the A_b attitudes that they do but also for controlling or influencing behaviour by altering controllable external variables that are linked to these beliefs.

1.4.3 Search and Elaboration: Identifying Salient Beliefs

Having chosen TRA as my basic framework for my theoretical model, my next step was the important one of identifying the salient beliefs that function as determinants of Attitude Toward Using a target system. The Theory of Reasoned Action draws a key distinction between object-based beliefs, which are perceived attributes of the attitude object, and behaviour-based beliefs, which are the subjective probability of salient consequences resulting from performing the behaviour. Object-based beliefs are the antecedents of A_o and should therefore not be expected to explain TRA's A_b construct. Instead, to use TRA the research should identify and include the salient behavioural beliefs. The fact that MIS implementation studies mostly used object-based beliefs and not behaviour-based beliefs is a possible explanation for why the prediction of behaviour was so often non-significant. TRA methodology stipulates that salient behavioural beliefs should be elicited for each study by conducting interviews with representative members of the subject population from which the sample for the study is drawn. Subjects are asked to list the advantages, disadvantages and any other consequences they associate with the behaviour, and their responses are used to identify typically five to nine salient beliefs to include in the model for that specific context.

A goal for TAM was to identify a priori the general salient beliefs that would be relevant for a broad range of end-user systems. This a priori approach is quite different from the TRA approach of eliciting salient beliefs anew for each new data collection effort. The a prior approach has the advantages of allowing for the development of (a) strong theoretical rationale for the selected general beliefs and (b) valid and reliable measures that could be used straight away by researchers and practitioners without redoing the belief identification process each time.

Another key goal for TAM is to be a motivational model of the user that traces the influence of system design features (functional and interface characteristics) on user motivation and subsequent system usage behaviour, as illustrated on Fig. 1.2. Therefore, particular emphasis is placed on identifying salient beliefs that can be influenced by the choice of design features, and that mediate between design features and attitude toward using in a causal chain.

My search and elaboration processes for salient beliefs involved iteratively navigating back and forth between four domains of thought (see Fig. 1.3):

- Current practices – documenting best current practices for designing and developing successful new end-user information systems, in particular examining user-centred development.
- Prior research – analysing the "cumulative tradition" of previous studies related to user acceptance of information systems to establish the frontier of knowledge as a baseline for a new contribution; this included three distinct literature streams: MIS field studies of system implementation, MIS lab studies, and Human Factors lab studies.
- Theoretical foundations – studying theory from neighbouring "reference disciplines" that might be imported and tailored to provide strong theoretical rationale for TAM to make a new contribution; reference disciplines included attitude theory, work motivation theory from management, self-efficacy theory from psychology, behavioural decision theory, diffusion of innovations and others.

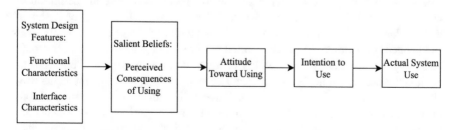

Fig. 1.2 Identifying salient beliefs for TAM

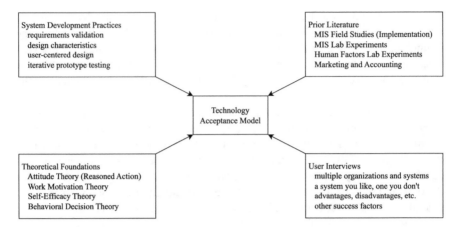

Fig. 1.3 Search and elaboration processes in developing TAM

- User interviews – conducting field interviews of end-users of information systems regarding their experiences accepting or rejecting new systems and learning more about the processes being used to design, test, select and implement them.

1.4.4 System Development Practices

First and foremost, TAM should be a practical tool that can be used by system developers to evaluate the potential user acceptance of a new system project beginning from the earliest stages of development. At an abstract level, system design and development can be viewed as the selection and construction of design features for a new system, including functional and interface characteristics. Many design choices are made very early in the development process. TAM is intended as a tool for validating that design choices are favourable for enhancing user acceptance. Therefore, it needs to be simple enough to conveniently use iteratively at different stages in development projects, and it should provide valid actionable guidance for design choices along the way.

Traditional waterfall development methodologies often fail because the requirements established toward the beginning of the project, including the definition of what problem the system is intended to solve and what functionality it should include, lead to a final system that is misaligned with users' true requirements. This can happen for a variety of reasons. Initial requirements gathered from users could be simply incorrect due to poor ability of users to correctly express their needs or communication problems between users and systems analysts. Requirements usually take the form of abstract statements that are difficult to verify in terms of confirming that the resulting system will have the right capability. Requirements are ambiguous, so decisions made regarding the translation of requirements into working system functionality can introduce a drift away from true needs. Requirements are often dynamically changing over the time course of a project, widening the gap between the original and current requirements.

For various reasons, therefore, initial requirements are imperfect for accurately identifying and managing project scope. Pressures on project managers to keep projects on time and underbudget motivate them to minimize scope drift and feature creep. Further exacerbating the situation is the fact the many project managers are measured and rewarded based on producing a deliverable that matches the specified requirements, irrespective of whether the requirements are correct or whether the final system will be accepted by users. User testing focuses on conformance to specifications, and actual workplace acceptance is typically "out of scope" for the project manager.

Projects can get significantly off-track regarding user acceptance, and tools are needed to detect when that happens and take corrective action. If changes are needed to the requirements or specifications for a system, the earlier in the project those are made the better. Earlier in the project much less time and money has been expended, so changes will result in less waste. Changes to scope are much more feasible early in a project.

In the early 1980s, user-centred design emerged as a paradigm shift for designing successful end-user systems. Early engagement with users and empirical testing of iterative evolving prototypes can go a long way toward reducing the gap between system functionality and user needs. When considering the advantages of user-centred design compared to traditional waterfall development, the idea of relevant functionality is at the heart of the issue. I use the term functionality to refer to the functional characteristics defining what the system can do for the user, in contrast to interface characteristics that define how the user will interact with the system. To me, requirements translate to functionality, and correct requirements translate to useful functionality. A system with functionality that is relevant for them will help them achieve their goals and enhance their performance. A system with relevant functionality will therefore be perceived as useful and will be likely to be accepted by users to my thinking. I find it intuitive and logical that perceived usefulness will be perhaps the most important factor driving user acceptance. And the most effective way to create a system perceived as useful is to make sure it has relevant functionality. I draw a key distinction between functionality and relevant functionality. Many systems fail to gain user acceptance despite offering a tremendous amount of functionality; the problem is the functionality is not relevant.

Advocates of user-centred design are often HCI specialists. Naturally, they are focused on system usability, and the usability metrics they favour for empirically testing prototypes are often slanted toward ease of use of the interface more so than relevance of the functionality. I highly appreciate the importance of a user-friendly interface. A poor interface could be the pivotal factor that determines acceptance or rejection of a system that would provide relevant functionality to users if accepted. However, I consider relevant functionality to be a more primary issue than a usable interface. Users will not likely accept and use a system with a very usable interface if it does not provide relevant functionality. Many users will tolerate a less than optimal user interface to access functionality that is highly relevant. I believe perceived usefulness and perceived ease of use can be influenced by the choice of functional and interface characteristics, respectively. Further, I consider perceived usefulness and ease of use to both function as determinants of A_b, and therefore are links in the causal chain linking system design features to user acceptance.

TAM was intended as a tool that could be added to the toolbox of HCI practitioners so that they could more fully evaluate user acceptance criteria alongside traditional usability criteria.

1.5   Specifying the Model Including Design Characteristics

The proclamation of the Technology Acceptance Model (TAM) took place in Fred Davis's 1986 Ph.D. dissertation at the Massachusetts Institute of Technology (MIT) (Davis, 1986). This crucial step not only established TAM's theoretical foundation but also introduced it to the scientific community, signifying a pivotal moment in Fred's academic journey.

The proposed model is illustrated in Fig. 1.4, where arrows indicate causal relationships. According to the model, a potential user's overall attitude toward using a given system is hypothesized to be a major determinant of whether or not the potential user actually uses it. Attitude toward using is, in turn, influenced by two major

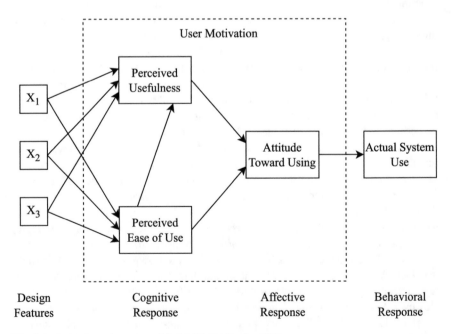

Fig. 1.4 Technology Acceptance Model, TAM. (Davis, 1986)

beliefs – perceived usefulness and perceived ease of use. Perceived ease of use is posited to have a causal effect on perceived usefulness. Design features directly influence perceived usefulness and perceived ease of use. As design features fall into the category of external variables, they are not theorized to have any direct effect on attitude or behaviour; instead, their affect is indirect, operating through perceived usefulness and perceived ease of use. Consistent with the Theory of Reasoned Action (Fishbein & Ajzen, 1975), the relationships within the model are theorized to be linear.

Actual System Use refers to an individual's actual direct usage of the given system in the context of his or her job. Thus, use is a repeated, multiple-act behavioural criterion that is specific with respect to target (specified system), action (actual direct usage) and context (in person's job) and non-specific with respect to the time frame. *Attitude Toward Using* refers to the degree of evaluative affect that an individual associates with using the target system in his or her job. Therefore, the definition and measurement of attitude corresponds in specificity with the definition of the behavioural criterion, as recommended by Ajzen and Fishbein (1977). *Perceived Usefulness* is defined as "the degree to which an individual believes that using a particular system would enhance his or her job performance". *Perceived Ease of Use* is defined as "the degree to which an individual believes that using a particular system would be free of physical and mental effort".

Perceived ease of use is hypothesized to have a significant direct effect on perceived usefulness, as a system that is easier to use is expected to enhance job performance (i.e. greater usefulness) for the user, assuming all other factors remain equal. Given that a non-trivial fraction of a user's total job content is dedicated to physically using the system itself, increased productivity in this aspect, resulting from greater ease of use, contributes to an overall boost in productivity for the user. Thus, the design characteristics of the system (represented by x_1, x_2 and x_3) may indirectly influence usefulness by impacting ease of use.

Closing the introductory chapter, we stand on the threshold of an exciting exploration into the realm of user acceptance. TAM, both simple and powerful, has proven its worth over more than three decades as a leading theory. As we embark on this journey, it becomes evident that despite various extensions (known as "TAM++"), the core TAM model's basic beliefs – perceived usefulness and perceived ease of use – remain unchanged. Like a crystal ball guiding us through the labyrinth of user acceptance, TAM provides the clarity needed to foresee, comprehend and enhance user interactions with technology. Through thorough validation and extension, TAM has demonstrated its resilience, providing valuable insights into the intricacies of user behaviour. TAM serves as a reliable tool for predicting, explaining and enhancing user acceptance across diverse technologies. Its enduring significance lies in its ability to guide us through the complexities of user behaviour, offering a clear lens to understand and improve technology adoption. Explore the evolving landscape of TAM and its extensions in the upcoming chapters, where we uncover the fundamental principles that continue to shape our understanding of user acceptance.

References

Ajzen, I., & Fishbein, M. (1977). Attitude-behavior relations: A theoretical analysis and review of empirical research. *Psychological Bulletin, 84*(5), 888–918. https://doi. org/10.1037/0033-2909.84.5.888

Bostrom, R. P., & Heinen, J. S. (1977). MIS problems and failures: A socio-technical perspective. Part I: The causes. *MIS Quarterly, 1*(3), 17. https://doi.org/10.2307/248710

Davis, F. D. (1986). *A technology acceptance model for empirically testing new end-user information systems: Theory and results.* Doctoral dissertation. MIT Sloan School of Management. https://dspace.mit.edu/handle/1721.1/15192

Davis, F. D. (1989). Perceived usefulness, perceived ease of use, and user acceptance of information technology. *MIS Quarterly, 13*(3), 319–340. https://www.jstor.org/stable/249008

Davis, F. D., Bagozzi, R. P., & Warshaw, P. R. (1989). User acceptance of computer technology: A comparison of two theoretical models. *Management Science, 35*(8), 982–1003. http://www.jstor.org/stable/2632151

Fishbein, M., & Ajzen, I. (1975). *Belief, attitude, intention and behavior: An introduction to theory and research.* Addison-Wesley.

Ginzberg, M. J. (1975). A critical survey of implementation research (CISR working paper). MIT.

Gould, J., & Lewis, C. (1985). Designing for usability: Key principles and what designers think. *Communications of the ACM, 28*(3), 300–311. https://doi.org/10.1145/3166.3170

ISO 9241-11:2018 *Ergonomics of human-system interaction – Part 11: Usability: Definitions and concepts.* International Organization for Standardization. https://www.iso.org/standard/63500.html

Keen, P. G. W. (1980, December). *MIS Research: Reference disciplines and cumulative tradition.* In E. McLean (Ed.), Proceedings of the first international conference on information systems, pp. 9–18.

Keen, P. G. W., & Scott Morton, M. S. (1978). *Decision support systems: An organizational perspective.* Addison-Wesley.

Smith, K. G., & Hitt, M. A. (Eds.). (2005). *Great minds in management: The process of theory development.* Oxford University Press.

Swanson, E. B. (1988). *Information system implementation: Bridging the gap between design and utilization.* Irwin.

Chapter 2
Evolution of TAM

Abstract The chapter traces the evolution of the Technology Acceptance Model (TAM) and underscores its consistent efficacy in predicting user acceptance across diverse technologies over more than three decades. Exploring beyond TAM research, alternative approaches aim to enrich our understanding of primary dependent constructs, specifically behavioural intentions and the actual behaviour (i.e. adoption) of technology. The chapter investigates the proliferation of selected TAM-related behavioural intention models and presents several integrated theoretical approaches. Additionally, it provides a chronological account of the era, illustrating interconnected relationships among the most influential theories and models in the field. Building on three dimensions of influence, this work systematically categorizes additional determinants of behavioural intention derived from various TAM extensions ("TAM++"). Notably, these new variables manifest and align with trends in the evolving landscape of emerging technologies, emphasizing TAM as a powerful and extensively validated theory. Its versatility is apparent across a broad spectrum of technological solutions, systems, environments, tools, applications, services and devices, as exemplified by numerous real-world applications explored in the chapter. TAM establishes itself as a simple and practical tool for delineating the determinants of technology adoption, proving effective even when integrated with well-established theories from related disciplines, thus spanning diverse multidisciplinary domains.

Keywords Chronological evolution · Technology Acceptance Model · TAM · Hybrid models · TAM++ · Triad of predictors · Behavioural intention · Moderators · Applications

© The Author(s), under exclusive license to Springer Nature
Switzerland AG 2024
F. D. Davis, A. Granić, *The Technology Acceptance Model*, Human–Computer
Interaction Series, https://doi.org/10.1007/978-3-030-45274-2_2

2.1   Proliferation and Consolidation of Behavioural Intention Models

2.1.1   Augmented TAM (A-TAM)

The Technology Acceptance Model (TAM), originally proposed by Davis in 1986, primarily focuses on the perceived usefulness and perceived ease of use of a technology as key determinants of technology adoption. However, TAM does not incorporate the influence of social beliefs and control beliefs on behaviour, which have been empirically shown to exert a significant impact on technology usage behaviour. These factors are integral components of Ajzen's Theory of Planned Behavior (TPB) (Ajzen, 1985, 1991), where social influences, often referred to as subjective norms, are conceptualized as determinants of behavioural intention, and perceived behavioural control is recognized as a determinant of both behavioural intention and actual behaviour.

Recognizing the limitations of TAM in capturing the broader range of determinants influencing technology adoption, Taylor and Todd (1995b) extended the model by incorporating subjective norm and perceived behavioural control. This augmentation resulted in a more comprehensive framework for assessing the key determinants of technology usage behaviour. The revised model has been referred to in the literature as the *Augmented Technology Acceptance Model* (A-TAM) and is also occasionally denoted as the *Combined TAM and TPB* (C-TAM-TPB). This integration of TAM and TPB constructs, as illustrated in Fig. 2.1, has provided researchers and practitioners with a more sophisticated understanding of the complex interplay between cognitive, social and control factors in shaping individuals' decisions to adopt technology.

2.1.2   Extended TAM (TAM2)

In light of the consistent findings that perceived usefulness plays a pivotal role in shaping the intention to use technology (Davis, 1989; Davis et al., 1989), Venkatesh and Davis (2000) proposed an elaboration of the Technology Acceptance Model (TAM) referred to as *Extended TAM*, TAM2. Building upon the foundation of TAM, TAM2 introduces additional theoretical constructs aimed at explaining the determinants of perceived usefulness and usage intentions through the lens of both social influence processes and cognitive instrumental processes (see Fig. 2.2).

TAM2 encompasses the influence of three interrelated social forces that impact individuals when they are confronted with the decision to embrace or reject a new technological system: subjective norm, voluntariness and image. In addition to elucidating the social influence processes that shape perceived usefulness and usage intentions, the authors posit four cognitive instrumental determinants that further elaborate on perceived usefulness: job relevance, output quality, result

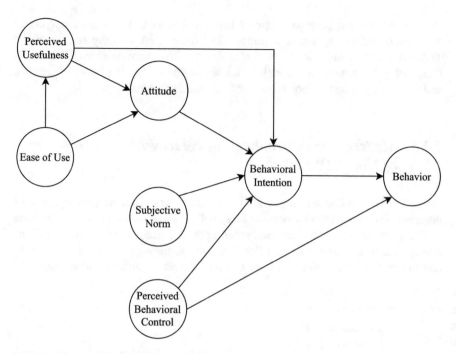

Fig. 2.1 Augmented Technology Acceptance Model, A-TAM. (Taylor & Todd, 1995b)

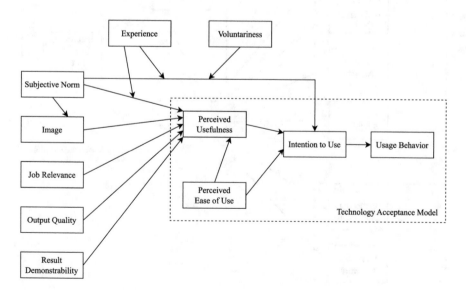

Fig. 2.2 Technology Acceptance Model 2, TAM2. (Venkatesh & Davis, 2000)

demonstrability and perceived ease of use. Furthermore, the model incorporates experience and voluntariness as moderating factors. Noteworthy findings from TAM2 research include the moderation of the subjective norm-perceived usefulness relationship by experience, as well as the significant influence of both experience and voluntariness on the subjective norm-intention relationship.

2.1.3   Model of the Determinants of Perceived Ease of Use (MDPEU)

While TAM2 (Venkatesh & Davis, 2000) explained the overarching determinants of perceived usefulness, the *Theoretical Model of the Determinants of Perceived Ease of Use* (Venkatesh, 2000) has expounded upon the general determinants of perceived ease of use, as depicted in Fig. 2.3. Two primary categories of antecedents contributing to perceived ease of use can be delineated: anchors and adjustments.

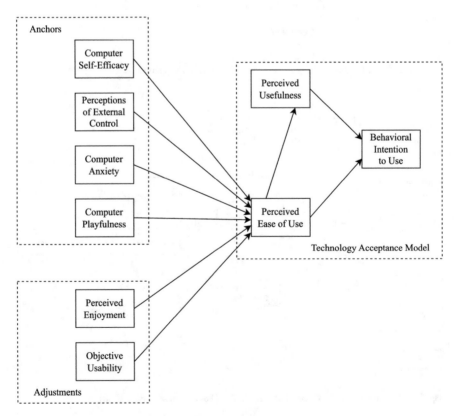

Fig. 2.3 The theoretical model of the determinants of perceived ease of use, MDPEU. (Venkatesh, 2000)

Anchors encompass broad beliefs regarding computers and computer usage, largely grounded in prior experience. Conversely, adjustments encompass beliefs shaped through direct interaction with the target system. In both these categories, various determinants, primarily drawn from prior research concerning the identification of antecedents to perceived ease of use (Davis et al., 1992), have been posited.

To be specific, control is separated into perceptions of internal control, encapsulated by computer self-efficacy, and perceptions of external control, represented by facilitating conditions. Intrinsic motivation is conceptually framed as computer playfulness, while emotion is characterized as computer anxiety. These constructs – computer self-efficacy, facilitating conditions, computer playfulness and computer anxiety – constitute system-independent anchoring constructs and serve as foundational elements, significantly influencing the formation of perceived ease of use, especially during the initial phases of user engagement with a system. As user experience with the system grows, certain adjustments come into play. Objective usability, perceptions of external control (pertaining specifically to the system in question) and the perceived enjoyment derived from system usage emerge as adjustments stemming from the user-system interaction. These adjustments exert an added influence on the system-specific perception of ease of use.

2.1.4 Technology Acceptance Model 3 (TAM3)

Venkatesh and Davis (2000) identified the overarching determinants of perceived usefulness, while Venkatesh (2000) delineated the general determinants of perceived ease of use. These two models were developed independently, and little is known about potential interplay between them. Specifically, it remains an open question as to whether the determinants of perceived usefulness may influence perceived ease of use, or vice versa. In response to this gap in knowledge, Venkatesh and Bala (2008) initiated and carried out the integration of TAM2 (Venkatesh & Davis, 2000) and MDPEU (Venkatesh, 2000), giving rise to an integrated framework known as the *Technology Acceptance Model 3* (TAM3). As illustrated in Fig. 2.4, TAM3 offers a "comprehensive nomological network" encompassing the determinants of individual-level adoption and utilization of information technology (IT). Importantly, TAM3 introduces three pivotal relationships that had not been empirically explored in the preceding models. The authors propose that experience serves as a moderating factor in the relationships between perceived ease of use and perceived usefulness, computer anxiety and perceived ease of use as well as perceived ease of use and behavioural intention.

TAM3 places distinct emphasis on the unique roles and processes associated with perceived usefulness and perceived ease of use. It postulates that the determinants affecting perceived usefulness will not exert influence on perceived ease of use and conversely. Furthermore, TAM3 posits that as experience with a system accumulates, the impact of perceived ease of use on behavioural intention will decrease, while the impact of perceived ease of use on perceived usefulness

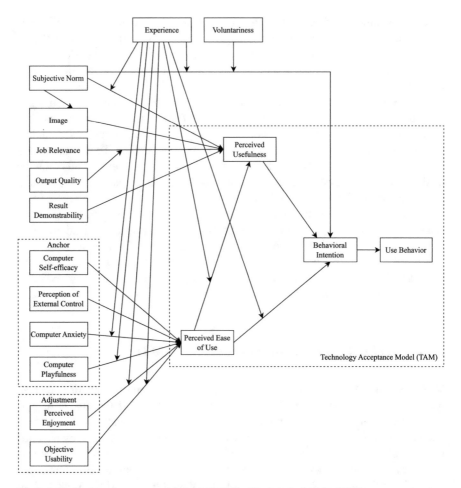

Fig. 2.4 Technology Acceptance Model 3 (TAM3). (Venkatesh & Bala, 2008)

will strengthen. This highlights the lasting significance of perceived ease of use as a user response to information technology, even when users possess substantial hands-on experience.

2.1.5   Chronological Representation of the Era

Beyond the extensive body of research dedicated to the Technology Acceptance Model (TAM), with specific emphasis on the determinants of perceived usefulness and perceived ease of use, the proliferation and consolidation of research investigating acceptance and adoption theories have produced various alternative approaches. These perspectives aim to enhance our comprehension of the primary dependent constructs of interest, specifically behavioural intentions and the actual behaviour (i.e. adoption) of technology.

In this context, the following provides a concise overview of the most influential theories and models related to technology adoption at the individual level. Figure 2.5 provides a chronological representation and an illustrative summary of the interconnected relationships among these approaches in the context of technology acceptance and adoption. This visual representation offers valuable insights into the extensive research conducted in the field over the course of more than half a century.

The theoretical approaches presented are as follows (listed in chronological order):

1. Innovation Diffusion Theory, IDT (Rogers, 1962, 1995).
2. Theory of Reasoned Action, TRA (Fishbein & Ajzen, 1975).
3. Theory of Interpersonal Behavior, TIB (Triandis, 1980).
4. Theory of Planned Behavior, TPB (Ajzen, 1985, 1991).
5. Social Cognitive Theory, SCT (Bandura, 1986).
6. Technology Acceptance Model, TAM (Davis, 1986, 1989).
7. Model of Personal Computer Utilization, MPCU (Thompson et al., 1991).
8. Perceived Characteristics of Innovating, PCI (Moore & Benbasat, 1991).
9. Motivational Model, MM (Davis et al., 1992).
10. Computer Self-Efficacy Model, CSEM (Compeau & Higgins, 1995).
11. Decomposed Theory of Planned Behavior, DTPB (Taylor & Todd, 1995a).

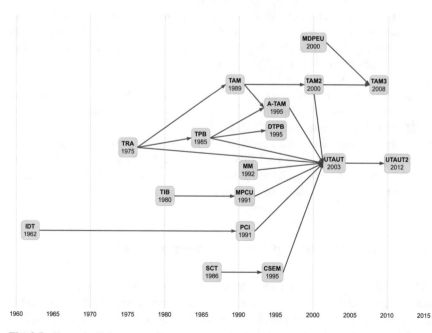

Fig. 2.5 Chronological account of the era and overview of interrelationships among influential theories and models of technology acceptance and adoption (Granić, 2023)

12. Augmented TAM, A-TAM (Taylor & Todd, 1995b), sometimes referred to as the Combined TAM and TPB, C-TAM-TPB.
13. Extended TAM, TAM2 (Venkatesh & Davis, 2000).
14. Model of the Determinants of Perceived Ease of Use, MDPEU (Venkatesh, 2000).
15. Unified Theory of Acceptance and Use of Technology, UTAUT (Venkatesh et al., 2003).
16. Technology Acceptance Model 3, TAM3 (Venkatesh & Bala, 2008).
17. Extended UTAUT, UTAUT2 (Venkatesh et al., 2016).

For a more in-depth exploration, you can refer to the systematic presentation of advancements in the realm of individual technology adoption as presented in Granić (2023). Granić's study does not intend to compare the relative strength of the most influential models or recommend one model's superiority over another. Instead, it provides a chronological account of the evolution of this field, offering an overview of the interrelationships among 17 widely applied models at the individual level.

Beyond the introduced well-established theoretical approaches, a substantial and diverse array of additional models and theories have been developed to enhance our understanding of the key dependent factors under investigation. These factors encompass conscious decisions or plans to engage in a specific behaviour (behavioural intention), the behaviour itself (adoption) as well as its sustained and continued use (post-adoption). These perspectives can be broadly categorized into three groups:

– Additional theoretical viewpoints pertaining to individual technology adoption that do not exhibit direct relational linkages with the most influential theories and models mentioned earlier, for example, *Theory of Trying* (TofT) (Bagozzi & Warshaw, 1990), *Task-Technology Fit* (TTF) (Goodhue & Thompson, 1995) and *Technology Readiness* (TR) (Parasuraman, 2000).
– Models and theories addressing individual post-adoption phases, such as *Expectation-Confirmation Theory* (ECT) (Oliver, 1980), *Information Systems Success Model* (ISSM) (DeLone & McLean, 1992) and *Expectation-Confirmation Model* (ECM) (Bhattacherjee, 2001).
– Numerous extensions and modifications to established adoption theories and models, as well as integrated (hybrid) approaches developed to enhance the explanatory power of each individual one; some of these integrated approaches are presented in the following section.

2.2 Advancing the Explanatory Power of TAM

With the aim of providing a comprehensive portrayal of the current research landscape within the domain of the Technology Acceptance Model (TAM), this section introduces a range of theoretical hybrid approaches. Specifically, to enhance explanatory power, particularly across diverse application domains, TAM has been integrated with other models and theories of technology adoption such as Theory of

Planned Behaviour (TPB), Unified Theory of Acceptance and Use of Technology (UTAUT), Social Cognitive Theory (SCT) and Technology Readiness (TR) and post-adoption such as Information System Success Model (ISSM) and Expectation–Confirmation Theory (ECT), as well as with several theoretical perspectives from other disciplines, including Flow Theory (FT), Protection Motivation Theory (PMT), the Push-Pull-Mooring (PPM) model, Health Belief Model (HBM), Uses and Gratifications Theory (UGT) and Self-Determination Theory (SDT), among others.

This study revealed that the Technology Acceptance Model (TAM), a notably robust framework demonstrably relevant across diverse technologies and individual contexts (as evidenced by recent reviews in the technology adoption domain (Al-Emran & Granić, 2021; Granić, 2022), has demonstrated efficacy in predicting user acceptance, even when combined with a spectrum of alternative theoretical perspectives.

By encompassing a variety of hybrid approaches, the intention here is to provide a more inclusive understanding of the TAM model. The introduction of a diverse range of hybrid models, identified through conducted systematic review or accumulated by the authors themselves, strives to capture the multifaceted nature of this domain. This also underscores the sustained relevance and impact of TAM within the technology acceptance and adoption field, even when integrated with other models or theories. While acknowledging that the presented works represent a selective compilation, it is crucial to recognize the existence of alternative contributions and relevant research endeavours. The adoption of this deliberate approach serves as an initial point for exploration, acknowledging the potential for diverse perspectives and interpretations based on different selections.

The subsequent discussion presents a range of illustrative hybrid methodologies and relevant instances of research spanning diverse multidisciplinary domains, as also depicted in Fig. 2.6.

– *Theory of Planned Behaviour* (TPB) (Ajzen, 1985, 1991), which states that behaviour is a direct function of behavioural intention and perceived behavioural control, is used with TAM to investigate the online shopping continuance intentions of older adults in the United States (Wu & Song, 2021), to propose and validate an unsafe behaviour model that provides understanding of how workers' attitude and perception factors would predict errors and violations at nuclear power plants (Zhang et al., 2020), to study factors that affect the acceptance of health information technology by patients with chronic diseases performing self-management at home (Liu et al., 2022) as well as to identify aspects that affect the adoption of mobile learning at the university level and to explain how perceptions influence the adoption of m-learning among students (Gómez-Ramirez et al., 2019).
– *Unified Theory of Acceptance and Use of Technology* (UTAUT) (Venkatesh et al., 2003), a rich theoretical approach to explaining behavioural intentions and technology use, is combined with TAM to explore universities lecturers' opinions of variables influencing actual blackboard use, as well as their desire to utilize

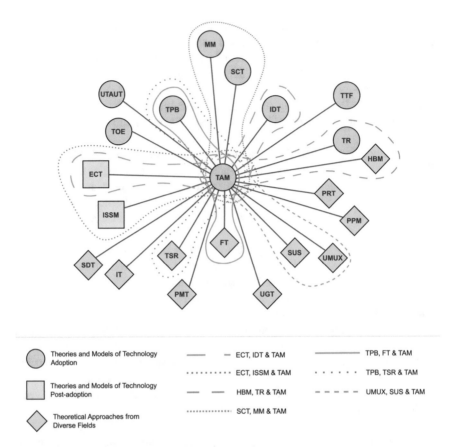

Fig. 2.6 Integrated theoretical approaches: understanding TAM in multidisciplinary domains

the lesson plan in learning and teaching during the COVID-19 Pandemic (Almogren, 2022).

- *Innovation Diffusion Theory* (IDT) (Rogers, 1962, 1995), one of the most popular models for studying the adoption and use of innovations at both individual and organizational levels, is combined with TAM in a research framework that aims to explain customer acceptance of advanced mobile services (López-Nicolás et al., 2008), to investigate the factors that affect the adoption of products based on haptic technology, such as driving simulation games or home entertainment devices with haptic technology (Jongchul & Sung-Joon, 2014) as well as to examine the motivation of the consumers' acceptance of the mobile technology to access tourism products and services focusing on a developing country, Pakistan (Gu et al., 2019).

- *Task-Technology Fit* (TTF) (Goodhue & Thompson, 1995), a model that explains the correlation between individuals' performance and information technologies, is integrated with TAM to propose a unified model that provides a more comprehensive understanding of the determinants of users' intention to use wireless technology in organizations (Yen et al., 2010), to investigate how students perceive the use of video technology and contents for the purpose of online learning in the COVID-19 era (Pal & Patra, 2021) or to study students' continuance intentions in using Massive Open Online Courses (MOOCs) in China (Wu & Chen, 2017).

- *Motivational Model* (MM) (Davis et al., 1992), which emphasizes the importance of motivational beliefs in shaping users' intentions to use technology and proposes that user acceptance of technology is influenced by motivational factors, including intrinsic and extrinsic motivation, is combined with TAM to understand citizens' preferences to use different types of interfaces for sharing information in a smart city project (Rebelo et al., 2018).

- *Social Cognitive Theory* (SCT) (Bandura, 1986), one of the strongest theories of human behaviour which posits that humans are influenced by the reciprocal interactions between cognitive processes, social factors and environmental determinants, is integrated with TAM to evaluate the students' happiness and real use of the m-learning system in higher education (Almogren & Aljammaz, 2022). Once again, SCT is integrated with TAM and MM in a study designed to examine the factors that influence students' intentions to continue using blogs for learning (Ifinedo, 2017).

- *Technology Readiness* (TR) (Parasuraman, 2000), a multiple item scale measuring readiness to adopt new technologies (through four dimensions: optimism and innovativeness, as drivers of technology readiness and discomfort and insecurity as barriers), is combined with TAM to explain the adoption of Industry 4.0 based on various technologies such as big data, cloud, industrial internet, simulation, augmented reality, additive manufacturing, cybersecurity, advanced manufacturing and the like (Castillo-Vergara et al., 2022).

- *Technology-Organization-Environment* (TOE) *Framework* (Tornatzky & Fleischer, 1990), one of leading theories which considers three key dimensions used to understand and analyse the adoption and implementation of new technology within organizations, is integrated with TAM to evaluate new decision factors which affect users' behaviour intention and actual usage towards e-banking (Kimiagari & Baei, 2022), as well as to examine influential factors in the acceptance of digital advertizing policy by Korean out-of-home adverting firms in the digital transformation process (Cho et al., 2022).

- *Information System Success Model* (ISSM) (DeLone & McLean, 1992), as an influential and robust theoretical foundation for the study of technology post-adoption, is combined with TAM to explore users' intention to use personalized location-based mobile tourism application (Chen & Tsai, 2019); to examine students' behavioural intentions to use social media, particularly their perceptions of academic performance and satisfaction (Al-Rahmi et al., 2021); as well as to understand the factors that influence consumer adoption and continued use of sports branded apps (Won et al., 2023).

- *Expectation–Confirmation Theory* (ECT) (Oliver, 1980), a widely used cognitive theory in the field of consumer satisfaction that seeks to explain post-adoption satisfaction as a function of expectations, perceived performance and disconfirmation of beliefs, is integrated with TAM to empirically examine what factors can potentially affect architectural designers' continuous use intention of building information modelling (Cui et al., 2021). Yet again, ECT is integrated with two other approaches, specifically TAM and ISSM, to examine and identify several factors as likely predictors of continuance intention in an e-learning context (Roca et al., 2006). Once more ECT is combined with TAM and IDT in a study which examines key factors affecting customer satisfaction and continuance intention to use e-wallet services and applications (Puspitasari et al., 2021).

- *Self-Determination Theory* (SDT) (Deci & Ryan, 1985), a theoretical approach widely used in studies of motivational behaviour, concerns the relationships among the social environment, psychological need, motivation, outcomes and well-being, is combined with TAM to examine the factors that predict Chinese students' continuance intention to use mobile learning for second language acquisition (He & Li, 2023).
- *Uses and Gratifications Theory* (UGT), a theory of mass communication that focuses on the needs, motivations and gratifications of media users and was first introduced in the 1940s when scholars began to study why people choose to consume different forms of media, is applied with TAM to identify key influencers of wearables adoption (Travers, 2015).
- *Push-Pull-Mooring* (PPM) *model* (Moon, 1995), a prevailing paradigm first used in the study of human migration that describes why people move from one place to another for a period of time, is used concurrently with TAM to build a conceptual model of the factors influencing the intention to use a metaverse educational application platform (Wang & Shin, 2022).
- *Flow Theory* (FT) (Csikszentmihalyi, 1975), a theory from positive psychology that describes a state in which a person is so involved in an activity that nothing else seems to matter, is combined with TAM in a theoretical framework designed to explain users' attitudes and behavioural intentions in a virtual reality surfing experience and its adoption in leisure and tourism (Huang et al., 2023). FT is yet again integrated with two other theoretical perspectives, TAM and TPB, to examine the intrinsic and extrinsic motivations that influence users' acceptance of instant messaging (Lu et al., 2009), as well as to examine the mechanism that explains young consumers' intention to perform online financial trading (Sharif & Naghavi, 2021).
- *Theory of Self-Regulation* (TSR) Bagozzi (1992), a theoretical approach that belongs to the domain of social psychology and organizational behaviour which forgoes parsimony to achieve a fuller explanation and understanding of social action and to enhance prediction, is integrated with TAM and TPB to examine the preferred reference book format among students at a government-linked boutique university in a developing country, Malaysia (Mustafa et al., 2021).
- *Health Belief Model* (HBM), one of the most widely used frameworks for studying health behaviour and designing health promotion interventions developed by social psychologists in the 1950s, is combined with TAM to examine the influence of perceived health risk and health consciousness on health-related Internet use (Ahadzadeh et al., 2015). Once again, HBM is integrated with TAM and TR

to understand the determinants of users' intention to continue using food delivery applications (Silva et al., 2022).
- *Protection Motivation Theory* (PMT), a theory postulated by R.W. Rogers (1975) to understand and explain how people make decisions about protective behaviours in the face of potential threats or risks, is combined with TAM to study students' behavioural intentions to adopt wearable technologies in learning activities, specifically smartwatch devices (Al-Emran et al., 2021).
- *Interactivity Theory* (IT), which focuses on the study of feedback as a concept and recognizes that new media tools have changed the way people communicate, is combined with TAM to examine the link between interactive features and personal cognition and to test key factors that affect users' intention to continue using mobile banking applications (Yin & Lin, 2022).
- *UMUX-LITE* (Lewis et al., 2013), as a short version of the *Usability Metric for User Experience* (UMUX) a four-item Likert scale used for the subjective assessment of an application's perceived usability; *System Usability Scale* (SUS) (Brooke, 1996), a ten-item low-cost usability scale used for global assessments of systems usability; as well as TAM are combined to investigate the relationships between measures of perceived usability and the two core variables of a modified version of the TAM (mTAM) (Lah et al., 2020).
- *Perceived Risk Theory* (PRT), an approach which revolves around the broader concept of perceived risk, a concept explored in different domains, such as marketing, consumer behaviour, psychology and decision-making research, is integrated with TAM to study the influential factors underlying consumers' intention to purchase fruits online (Wei et al., 2018), as well as to explore factors affecting citizens' intentions to use e-government in the Vietnamese context during the COVID-19 era (Nguyen, 2023).

2.3 The Search for Other Behavioural Intention Antecedents

As underscored by the extensive body of research, the Technology Acceptance Model (TAM) has established itself as a powerful and parsimonious way of delineating the antecedents of technology adoption. This model encapsulates these antecedents primarily through two crucial core determinants of user acceptance: perceived usefulness and perceived ease of use (Davis et al., 1989). These basic beliefs of the original TAM model subsequently shape attitudes toward usage, ultimately determining the behavioural intention to use. Over the course of more than three decades since TAM's introduction, numerous extensions with additional variables have aimed to deepen our understanding of usage determinants.

Building upon Eason's well-established ergonomic framework, which spans three decades and encompasses the facets of human, machine, task and environment (Eason, 1991), Granić's 2023 study introduced a *Triad of Predictors* with the goal of thematically categorizing the determinants of behavioural intention. Elaborating on these three dimensions of influence, this research systematically categorizes additional constructs (variables) derived from numerous proposed extensions of the Technology Acceptance Model, collectively referred to as "TAM++", in the following thematic manner:

- *User aspects* – this refers to specific traits or qualities of individual users that may influence their behaviours related to technology acceptance and adoption; it encompasses individual characteristics, user pleasure and perceived utility when adopting technology.
- *Task and technological aspects* – this group encompasses variables related to technological and task-related factors within the context of technology acceptance and adoption.
- *Social and environmental aspects* – this group includes variables related to social and environmental factors within the realm of technology acceptance and adoption.

It is important to mention that in the course of the categorization process, an issue of consideration emerges, as it warrants acknowledgment that certain variables may be amenable to multiple interpretive perspectives. For example, variable "job relevance", foreseen as an individual' perception regarding the extent to which a technology applies to their job, can be seen from both the user's perspective and the technological perspective.

Job relevance primarily deals with users' perceptions of how a technology aligns with their job roles and responsibilities. Users' attitudes, motivations and decisions to adopt a technology are influenced by how they perceive its relevance to their work. This user-centric viewpoint emphasizes the role of "job relevance" as a user-related factor. On the other hand, one could argue that "job relevance" could be viewed as a characteristic of the technology itself. Technologies designed for specific industries or job functions might inherently possess certain features that make them more relevant to those roles. In this sense, the technology's alignment with particular job contexts becomes a technological consideration. Taking both perspectives into account, it is possible to interpret "job relevance" as encompassing elements of both user-related and technological aspects. Thus, this aspect may depend on how the individual research study is framed and the specific technology acceptance model utilized.

Subsequently, in the following a thematical categorization of antecedents of behavioural intention is presented in chronological order, along with the original authors' corresponding definitions. The temporal sequence associated with the introduction of various antecedents of behavioural intention within the proposed extended versions of TAM is a subject of particular interest in the reviewed literature. It is notable to observe how these new variables manifest and adhere to prevailing patterns and trends in the evolving landscape of emerging technologies. Furthermore, it is of interest to observe how the academic community's areas of focus evolve over time, as they aim to predict user acceptance across a wide range of information and communication technology (ICT) products and services.

2.3.1   User Aspects

Individual Characteristics In the context of technology acceptance and adoption, individual characteristics refer to personal attributes, skills, beliefs or tendencies that influence how a person interacts with and perceives technology. This sub-category includes the following variables:

- *Self-efficacy* – an individual judgment of one's capability to use a technology to accomplish a particular task or job (Compeau & Higgins, 1995; Vijayasarathy, 2004; Chen et al., 2022; Zobeidi et al., 2023).
- *Prior usage* – the extent to which users use the current information systems (Jackson et al., 1997; Amoako-Gyampah, 2007).
- *Cognitive absorption* – the totality of an individual's experience with new software (Agarwal & Karahanna, 2000; Saadé & Bahli, 2005).
- *Voluntariness* – the extent to which potential adopters perceive the adoption decision to be non-mandatory (Venkatesh & Davis, 2000).
- *Trust* – a belief that others upon whom one depends, yet has little control over, will not take advantage of the situation by behaving opportunistically but, rather, will fulfil their expected commitments (Gefen et al., 2003; Pavlou, 2003; Gefen, 2004; Wu & Chen, 2005; Tung et al., 2009; Wu et al., 2011a, b; Yousafzai et al., 2010; Lee & Wan, 2010; Ooi & Tan, 2016; Beldad & Hegner, 2018; Sharma, 2019; Baby & Kannammal, 2020; Acikgoz & Perez Vega, 2022; Yu, 2022; Acharya & Mekker 2022; Xu et al., 2022; Ge et al., 2023).
- *Perceived risk* – an uncertainty regarding possible negative consequences of using a product or service (Featherman & Pavlou, 2003; Pavlou, 2003; Wu & Wang, 2005; Lee, 2009; Kwee-Meier et al., 2016; Sagheer et al., 2022; Girish et al., 2022).
- *Training* – a direct experience with the system (Amoako-Gyampah & Salam, 2004).
- *Age* – a period of human life, measured by years from birth (Lai & Li, 2005; Chen et al., 2022).
- *Gender* – a multifaceted social construct that encompasses the roles, behaviours, expectations, and identities associated with being male or female (Lai & Li, 2005).
- *Compatibility* – a degree to which an innovation is perceived as being consistent with the existing values, needs, and past experiences of potential adopters (Wu & Wang, 2005; Tung et al., 2009; Ooi & Tan, 2016; Choi, 2022).
- *Information technology competency* – a level of expertise in using information technology (IT) systems (Lai & Li, 2005).
- *Education level* – a highest level of a formal qualification or training the individual has attained (Gumussoy et al., 2007).
- *Intrinsic involvement* – the extent to which the object in question has personal relevance, psychological significance and significant consequences for the individual (Amoako-Gyampah, 2007; Leso & Cortimiglia, 2022).

- *Impulsiveness* – a tendency to act immediately, spontaneously, and unreflectively (Stern et al., 2008).
- *Perceived aesthetics* – a subjective perception of technology composed of pleasure and beauty based on intrinsic and extrinsic motivation (Tzou & Lu, 2009).
- *Concentration* – an ability to maintain focused attention and cognitive engagement while using a particular technology for a specific task or (Lu et al., 2009).
- *Positive mood* – one's feeling state or how one feels when performing some task or activity (Djamasbi et al., 2010).
- *Personality traits* – a quality or characteristic that distinguishes the character, action and attitude of a person (Svendsen et al., 2013).
- *(Autonomous, intrinsic) motivation* – the human behaviour motivated by internally induced incentives; an individuals' engagement in a physical activity purely for the pleasure and satisfaction derived from doing the activity per se (Joo & Sang, 2013; Sharma, 2019; Wang, Y. et al., 2022b).
- *Privacy concern* – a sensitivity for location identification in case of emergency and anonymous continuous locating (Kwee-Meier et al., 2016; Chang et al., 2016; Lin & Kim, 2016).
- *Flow* – a holistic experience when involved in the action (Chen et al., 2017; Ren et al., 2022).
- *Personal norms* – feelings of personal obligation to engage in a certain behaviour based on internalized values (Yoon, 2018).
- *Cybersickness* – a relatively common negative outcome of exposure to virtual environments (Sagnier et al., 2020).
- *Sense of direction* – an awareness of location or orientation; a verbal expression of people's estimation of their own spatial orientation abilities (Yang et al., 2021).
- *Distraction perception* – a perceived effects of distraction caused by navigation applications on individuals' vision, hearing, decision-making and behaviours (Yang et al., 2021).
- *Uncertainty avoidance* – the extent to which individuals in a society feel threatened by situations that are undefined, ambiguous and uncertain (Girish et al., 2022).
- *Privacy cynicism* – an attitude of uncertainty, powerlessness and mistrust towards the handling of personal data by online services, rendering privacy protection behaviour subjectively futile (Acikgoz & Perez Vega, 2022).
- *Employee factor* – skills related to the use of technology by employees (Tavakoli et al., 2023).
- *Internet anxiety* – an undesirable emotion a person can experience when working with technology (Zobeidi et al., 2023).

Pleasure As an important factor influencing the user's overall perception of the technology, the term "pleasure" refers to the emotional or experiential aspect of using technology. It encompasses the outlined variables:

- *Perceived enjoyment* – the extent to which the activity of using the computer is perceived to be enjoyable in its own right, apart from any performance consequences that may be anticipated (Davis et al., 1992; van der Heijden, 2004; Yu et al., 2005; Huang et al., 2007; Shin & Kim, 2008; Lee et al., 2019; Oyman et al., 2022).
- *Perceived fun* – the extent to which the activity of using a computer is perceived as enjoyable in its own right (Roberts & Henderson, 2000).
- (*Perceived*) *playfulness* – the question of how intrinsic motives affect the individual's acceptance of technology (Moon & Kim, 2001); the pedagogical learning appropriateness of teaching computer science with Augmented Reality based on cognitive-learning model (Papakostas et al., 2023).
- *User satisfaction* – the degree to which users are satisfied and pleased with their prior use of an information system (Lee & Lehto, 2013; Park & Kim, 2013; Park et al., 2014; Park & Kim, 2014; Yoon, 2016; Chang & Chen, 2018).
- *Hedonic motivation* – the fun or pleasure derived from using technology (Guest et al., 2018).

Utility As another significant factor influencing the user's perception of technology, the term "utility" refers to the perceived value and practical benefits of using technology. This sub-category covers the subsequent variables:

- *Perceived mobility* – user awareness of the mobility value of m-learning (Huang et al., 2007); the extent of user awareness of the mobility value of mobile services and systems (Park et al., 2014).
- *Perceived benefit* – value from a wider range of financial benefits, faster transaction speed and increased information transparency in internet banking (Lee, 2009); the role of hedonic benefits of advanced mobile technologies (Lopez-Nicolas et al., 2008).
- *Perceived financial cost* – user's perception of the magnitude of the costs using the system (monetary, stress and time) that add negative value to users when making a decision (Shin, 2009).
- *Educational quality* – the extent to which an information system managed to provide a conducive learning environment for learners in terms of collaborative learning (Mohammadi, 2015).
- *Content and information quality* – the quality of the information that the system generates and its usefulness for the user (Mohammadi, 2015).
- *Technical system quality* – a technical success and the accuracy and efficiency of the communication system that produces information (Mohammadi, 2015).
- *Service quality* – the quality of the support that users receive from the information system (Mohammadi, 2015; Park et al., 2015; Choi, 2022).
- *E-service quality* – how much an electronic or online system helps productivity and adequacy in conveyance of service (Ahmad et al., 2019).

2.3.2   Task and Technological Aspects

When users evaluate technology for adoption, they often consider how well it aligns with their specific tasks and whether it offers the technological features and capabilities that will make those tasks easier or more efficient. This category includes the listed variables:

- *Situational involvement* – the extent of participation in various activities related to technology development and implementation (Jackson et al., 1997); all activities, agreements and behaviours performed by the user during system development (Leso & Cortimiglia, 2022).
- *Perceived resources* – the extent to which an individual believes that she/he has the personal and organizational resources needed to use an information system, such as skills, hardware, software, money, documentation, data, human assistance and time (Mathieson et al., 2001).
- *Performance expectancy* – the degree to which an individual believes that using the system will help her/him to attain gains in job performance (Venkatesh et al., 2003; Guest et al., 2018).
- *Effort expectancy* – the degree of ease associated with the use of the system (Venkatesh et al., 2003; Guest et al., 2018).
- *Cost* – an amount that has to be paid or spent to buy or obtain equipment, access cost and transaction fees of mobile commerce (Wu & Wang, 2005).
- *Perceived availability* – users feeling that they can access the content at any place and at any time (Shin, 2009).
- *Job relevance* job fit (with use) – the extent to which an individual believes that using a technology can enhance the performance of his or her job (Kim & Garrison, 2009).
- *Wearability* – the interaction between the human body and the wearable object (Chang et al., 2016).
- *Convenience* – an availability, accessibility and agility of a product taking into consideration the time and effort exerted to attain it (Bassiouni et al., 2019).
- *Navigation application affinity* – the perceived importance of navigation applications and its content to individuals in their lives (Yang et al., 2021).
- *Technology awareness* – users' access to the available information about the benefits and potential risks and the strategies that are usually employed in adopting technology (Sagheer et al., 2022).
- *E-learning interactivity* – the interactive communication that happens between the instructor and students within an e-learning platform (Girish et al., 2022).
- *Perceived data privacy* – the degree to which an individual is concerned about the collection and use of his or her data (Acharya & Mekker, 2022).
- *Perceived data security* – the degree to which an individual is concerned about the unauthorized access and protection of data (Acharya & Mekker, 2022).
- *Relative advantage* – the degree to which using the innovation is perceived as being better than using its precursor (Choi, 2022).
- *Perceived informativeness* – adequate useful and reliable information in the application (Oyman et al., 2022).

– *Output quality* – the degree to which a person thinks or believes a system works satisfactorily; the level of positive effects of a person's use of an information system (Zobeidi et al., 2023).
– *Technological factors* – comparative advantage, complexity, testability, compatibility, technological infrastructure, security and privacy (Tavakoli et al., 2023).

2.3.3 Social and Environmental Aspects

Users often consider how technology aligns with their social and environmental context when making decisions about its adoption and use. As this involves elements or considerations related to broader societal and contextual conditions, this category covers the following variables:

– *Social norms* – collective representations of acceptable group conduct as well as individual perceptions of particular group conduct (organizational variable) (Lucas & Spitler, 1999; Chang & Chen, 2018; Beldad & Hegner, 2018; Mir & Padma, 2020).
– *Subjective norm* – the person's perception that most people who are important to her/him think she/he should or should not perform the behaviour in question (Venkatesh & Morris, 2000; Spacey et al., 2004; Wu & Chen, 2005; Gumussoy et al., 2007; Schepers & Wetzels, 2007; Lu et al., 2009; Pan & Jordan-Marsh, 2010; Choi & Chung, 2013; Chang et al., 2016; Xie et al., 2017; Yu & Huang, 2020).
– *Social influence* – the degree to which an individual perceives that important others believe he or she should use the new system (Venkatesh et al., 2003; Lopez-Nicolas et al., 2008; Shin, 2009; Kwee-Meier et al., 2016; Guest et al., 2018).
– *Normative beliefs* – beliefs about whether or not important referent groups or individuals would approve of the behaviour under study (Vijayasarathy, 2004).
– *Perceived reachability* – the individual's perception regarding the degree to which she/he can "reach" other individuals "anytime-and-anywhere" via mobile wireless technology (MWT) (Kim & Garrison, 2009).
– *Perceived ubiquity* – the individual's perception regarding the extent to which mobile wireless technology provides personalized and uninterrupted connection and communications between the individual and other individuals and/or networks (Kim & Garrison, 2009).
– *Facilitating conditions* – the degree to which an individual believes that an organizational and technical infrastructure exists to support use of the system(Pan & Jordan-Marsh, 2010).
– *Descriptive norms* – the people's perceptions of what most people do without imposing a judgment (Yoon, 2018).
– *Electronic word of mouth* –comments whether are positive or negative or likes to video clips on short video apps(Wang, C. et al., 2022a).

2.4   The Search for TAM Moderators

While the majority of TAM research has primarily concentrated on identifying antecedents of behavioural intention, there is a growing need to understand factors that
moderate relationships among the core determinants of user acceptance (the two
key drivers of user acceptance), as well as those that impact the model itself. Several
moderating factors for the basic beliefs of the core TAM model, namely perceived
usefulness and perceived ease of use, have been introduced, along with numerous
variables that moderate relationships among TAM constructs.

In the process of understanding gender differences in the context of individual
technology adoption and sustained usage in the workplace, Venkatesh and Morris
(2000) drew upon research regarding gender differences in the salience of outcomes
as determinants of behaviour. They introduced subjective norm as a new variable
into the Technology Acceptance Model (TAM), also examining *gender* and *experience* as moderators in the relationships among TAM's core constructs. The research
findings revealed that men place a greater emphasis on perceived usefulness when
making decisions about adopting new technology, both in the short and long term.
Conversely, perceived ease of use held greater importance for women, both following initial training and as they gained experience with the system over time.

Seeking to investigate the receptivity of college students toward acquiring basketball skills through metaverse technology, Ren et al. (2022) augmented the
Technology Acceptance Model (TAM) by introducing *gender* as a moderating element. Their findings illuminate that gender exerts a moderating influence on the
associations between perceived ease of use and behavioural intention, attitude and
behavioural intention, as well as the flow experience and attitude. On the other
hand, Cheng et al. (2015) sought to re-examine and incorporate several moderators,
including *gender*, *grade level* and *willingness to share*, in order to comprehend the
adoption of e-portfolios. The results empirically supported the validity of the TAM
instrument and clarified that the relationships among variables would not be influenced by individual characteristics such as gender, grade levels or varying degrees
of willingness to share.

Besides, Padilla-Melendez et al. (2013) argued that *gender* differences exist in
attitudes and intentions toward using the blended learning scenario. Their research
model integrated playfulness as a new variable in TAM. The primary contribution
of their study lies in providing evidence that gender differences exist in the impact
of playfulness on students' attitudes toward technology and their intention to use it.
For females, playfulness directly influences their attitude toward using the system,
while in males, this influence is mediated by perceived usefulness.

The moderating influence of individual factors such as *age*, *gender*, *subjective
technical confidence* and *computer expertise* in shaping the connection between
technical proficiency and the acceptance of computer-simulated personal digital
assistant devices was systematically investigated by Arning and Ziefle (2007).
The outcomes of their analysis unveiled associations between performance metrics
and the core constructs of the Technology Acceptance Model (TAM), with this

relationship more pronounced within the older demographic, particularly regarding performance and the perceived ease of use. Furthermore, Pan and Jordan-Marsh (2010) delved into the role of *age* as a moderator in the context of behavioural intention and the decision-making processes of older adults in adopting the Internet. The influence of *age* as a moderator was also examined in Nayak et al.'s (2010) study, which focused on the utilization of the Internet among elderly users. Their research revealed that good health, moderated by age, emerged as a robust predictor of Internet usage.

The examination of computer acceptance within diverse cultural contexts became the focal point of investigation in the study conducted by Alshare et al. (2011). Their research exposed that *national culture* plays a moderating role in the context of Technology Acceptance Model (TAM) constructs. Additionally, Wu, K. et al. (2011b) explored the moderating influences of *subject type* (students or non-students) and *context type* (commercial or non-commercial research settings) within the realm of e-commerce. Their findings indicated moderating effects for most relationships within the TAM framework. Besides, these authors delved into the role of *trust* as a moderator in shaping user behaviour online, with their results highlighting a significant influence of trust on various TAM constructs.

In an effort to investigate the determinants shaping farmers' decision-making processes concerning their engagement in rural tourism, the research conducted by Yu (2022) utilized the Technology Acceptance Model (TAM) as a framework to forecast and assess individual farmers' inclination and actions regarding participation in rural tourism. The findings revealed that *perceived risk* played a moderating role in the relationship between government trust and perceived usefulness in this context.

The primary aim of a recent study conducted by Ge et al. (2023) was to explain the underlying mechanisms governing the utilization of navigation systems and to analyse the psychological determinants impacting drivers' adoption of such systems. The research findings demonstrated that the status of being a professional driver (*professional driver status*) assumes a moderating role in the pathway from Technology Acceptance Model (TAM) variables and trust to the formation of positive attitudes.

An additional factor that serves as a moderator in the interplay among Technology Acceptance Model (TAM) constructs is the concept of *uniqueness*, denoting the intrinsic desire to perceive oneself as distinct from others. This facet was studied by Tzou and Lu (2009) in the context of fashion technology acceptance. Their investigation revealed that uniqueness played a moderating role in the relationship between pleasure, beauty and the intention to use fashion technology among the consuming public.

In addition, *personal innovativeness*, characterized as an individual's inclination to experiment with novel information technologies, has been identified as a moderator affecting the connection between travellers' attitudes and their behavioural intentions regarding the utilization of in-vehicle global positioning system (GPS) products, as documented by Chen and Chen (2011) in their research.

Yang and Yoo (2004) extended the Technology Acceptance Model framework by incorporating both affective and cognitive dimensions of attitude in the context of information systems usage. Their research yielded two principal findings. Firstly, they determined that within the realm of technology acceptance, affective and cognitive attitudes manifest as distinct sociopsychological variables. Secondly, they found that exclusively the *cognitive attitude* serves as a mediator in facilitating the influence of perceived usefulness and perceived ease of use on the adoption of information systems.

The findings from Saadé and Kira's (2006) research elucidated the interplay between *affect* and *computer anxiety* and their roles as moderators in shaping perceptions of ease of use and usefulness in the context of an online learning system. The results imply that affect and anxiety may coexist as influential factors on opposite ends of the TAM spectrum. Within this framework, *computer anxiety* is characterized as a concept-specific anxiety, given its association with an individual's interaction with computers. Meanwhile, the term "affective" pertains to an individual's emotional experiences encompassing feelings of joy, elation, pleasure, depression, distaste, discontentment or antipathy in relation to a specific behaviour or context.

Finally, Huang et al. (2003) aimed to investigate the moderating influence of *power distance*, a fundamental cultural or societal value within workplace contexts, on the relationship between subjective norms and the perceived usefulness of email. To achieve this, they expanded the universal applicability of the Technology Acceptance Model across diverse cultural settings by incorporating cultural influence into its theoretical framework. Their findings reveal that the interaction effect of power distance on user acceptance of email technology is substantial, and this is observed in its negative moderating impact on the relationship between subjective norms and perceived usefulness.

2.5 TAM in Various Contexts and Applications

Technology Acceptance Model (TAM) found extensive application both as a means to assess its relevance and to enhance its predictive efficacy. This model has gained widespread recognition for its validity and reliability in predicting user acceptance across a range of ICT products and services. This utilization encompasses a broad spectrum of technological solutions, interactive systems, environments, tools, applications, services and devices, all of which have been subjects of examination in the studies under consideration.

The progression of personal computers, coupled with the expansion of the Internet and the World Wide Web, has inspired various authors to formulate research models based on the Technology Acceptance Model to predict their adoption. Particularly, the World Wide Web (WWW) gathered early attention in the context of technology acceptance, as evidenced by studies conducted by Lederer et al. (2000)

and Moon and Kim (2001), while Alshare et al. (2011) examined the acceptance of personal computers. The evolving landscape of the WWW encouraged scholars like Shin and Kim (2008) and Alexandrakis et al. (2020) to pivot their TAM-focused research toward the domain of Web 2.0. Besides, in the context of predicting a user's intention to revisit a website, Castaneda et al. (2007) applied the TAM framework to assess a free-content website, considering the user's Internet and website experience.

Furthermore, Intranet and Internet technologies have drawn considerable scholarly examinations. Researchers such as Horton et al. (2001) and Lee and Kim (2009) delved into the extent of Intranet integration and usage within organizations. Several investigations have explored Internet utilization from the user's standpoint, as exemplified in studies conducted by Shih (2004), Spacey et al. (2004), Nayak et al. (2010) and Pan and Jordan-Marsh (2010).

The acceptance of e-mail technology has gathered significant scholarly attention, with studies conducted by Gefen and Straub (1997) and Burton-Jones and Hubona (2006). Moreover, Serenko (2008) contributed to this discourse by introducing and empirically substantiating a model elucidating user adoption patterns concerning e-mail notification interface agents, approached from the perspective of end-users.

Son et al. (2012) employed the Technology Acceptance Model to investigate the key factors influencing user satisfaction of mobile computing devices. Subsequently, Park and Kim (2014) extended their research to encompass mobile cloud computing services, while more recently, Tavakoli et al. (2023) adopted a cloud computing approach to explain the impact of artificial intelligence within the context of media.

In another study, Wu and Wang (2005) utilized TAM to predict the usage patterns of mobile commerce. Meanwhile, Lu et al. (2003) developed a technology acceptance model tailored to clarify the determinants shaping user acceptance of wireless Internet via mobile devices. Yoon and Kim (2007) formulated a TAM specifically tailored to wireless local area networks, while the research by Park and Kim (2013) centred on long-term evolution (LTE) services. In addition, Wu et al. (2011a, b) conducted a comparative analysis of two iterations of TAM with the aim of comprehending the factors that influence user intention to employ wireless technology within a workplace context.

Given the pervasive reliance of workplaces on Information Technology (IT) and its constantly expanding capabilities, the widespread adoption of IT within professional settings has been the subject of investigation through the lens of technology acceptance. This line of inquiry has been explored by researchers such as Roberts and Henderson (2000), McFarland and Hamilton (2006), and Guner and Acarturk (2020), shedding light on the broader landscape of IT integration in workplace environments. Additionally, a more focused analysis was conducted on Enterprise Resource Planning (ERP) technology, with Bueno and Salmeron (2008) and Amoako-Gyampah and Salam (2004) delving into the specifics of this technology's acceptance within organizational contexts.

In addition to these studies, the broader domain of Information Systems has gathered attention of Yang and Yoo (2004), as well as Leso and Cortimiglia (2022).

Besides, web-based ISs, examined by Yi and Hwang (2004) and Cheung and Sachs (2006), have all contributed to the discourse surrounding the adoption of information systems in various contexts.

Moreover, the Customer Relationship Management Information System (CRM IS) was studied in the research conducted by Tung et al. (2009), shedding light on the factors influencing its acceptance and implementation within organizational settings. Recognizing the paramount importance of security informatics, Hu et al. (2005) undertook an empirical evaluation of a TAM-based model to explicate the acceptance of information security technology, thereby contributing to our understanding of security technology adoption within the broader IT landscape.

With the increasing shift of money transactions and shopping to online platforms, there has been a growing scholarly interest in examining the acceptance of emerging modes of commerce. Many studies have probed into the adoption and usage behaviours associated with Internet banking services. For instance, Chan and Lu (2004), Lai and Li (2005), Yousafzai et al. (2010) as well as Nasri and Charfeddine (2012) have contributed to this discourse. In addition to Internet banking, researchers have explored the acceptance of online banking services, as evident in the work of Pikkarainen et al. (2004), Lee (2009) and Ahmad et al. (2019). Mobile banking has also garnered significant attention, as demonstrated by Sharma's research in 2019.

Furthermore, Ooi and Tan (2016) have developed a predictive model for assessing the acceptance of smartphone-based credit cards. The study by Yu et al. (2005) employed the Technology Acceptance Model (TAM) to explain the acceptance of electronically mediated commerce using interactive television (t-commerce), while Lee and Wan (2010) investigated the utilization of e-ticketing services. Vijayasarathy (2004) and Chiu et al. (2009) focused their research efforts on online shopping, while Gu et al. (2019) delved into mobile-based shopping. Stern et al. (2008) directed their attention to online auctions, examining the factors influencing user acceptance in this domain.

More recent investigations include the study by Sagheer et al. (2022), which explored the determinants affecting the acceptance of blockchain-based technology and cryptocurrencies for monetary transactions. In addition, Acikgoz and Perez Vega (2022) centred their research on consumer behaviours related to voice assistants in the context of commerce.

The predominant focus of scholarly investigations has centred on the application of the Technology Acceptance Model (TAM) within an educational context. Saadé and Bahli (2005), Zhang et al. (2008), and Farahat (2012) have all put forth TAM-based models for gauging acceptance levels in the context of online learning. Moreover, various researchers have undertaken the assessment of TAM's applicability within the context of e-learning practice, a term often used interchangeably, including Park et al. (2009), Lee et al. (2013), Mohammadi (2015), Baby and Kannammal (2020), Girish et al. (2022), and, most recently, Zobeidi et al. (2023).

Additionally, Huang et al. (2007) conducted a study aimed at formulating and validating the notion that TAM can effectively predict the acceptance of mobile learning (m-learning). The domain of mobile learning has also captured the attention of researchers such as Sanchez-Prieto et al. (2017). Efforts to enhance online learning experiences have resulted in the creation and evaluation of free Massive Open Online Courses (MOOCs) (Wu & Chen, 2017), as well as various platforms, notably Moodle (Sánchez & Hueros, 2010).

Besides, Cheung and Vogel (2013) extended the TAM to elucidate the factors influencing the acceptance of Google Applications in the context of collaborative learning. Also, the application of TAM in the field of teaching and learning has encompassed a spectrum of innovative technologies, spanning from web-based learning systems (Calisir et al., 2014) to technology designed to enhance the learning process through e-training (Zainab et al., 2017), teaching assistant robots (Park & Kwon, 2016), metaverse technology (Ren et al., 2022), virtual reality (Lin & Yeh, 2019; Lee et al., 2019) and, most recently, augmented reality (Papakostas et al., 2023).

The continuous advancement of healthcare technology, coupled with concerns regarding patient safety and the efficacy of medical treatments, has drawn an escalating level of attention to healthcare information systems. Consequently, numerous studies have been dedicated to the application of the Technology Acceptance Model (TAM) in elucidating user intentions concerning the adoption of clinical information systems. Contributions include the research conducted by Pai and Huang (2011) and Melas et al. (2011).

The utilization of TAM has been explored in the context of electronic healthcare records, as evidenced by the work of Egea and González (2011), as well as Razmak and Belanger (2018). In addition, several studies have investigated TAM's applicability in explaining physicians' acceptance of telemedicine technology within the healthcare sector, like the investigations conducted by Hu et al. (1999) and Chau and Hu (2002). Furthermore, recent research efforts have concentrated on the utilization of virtual reality games for rehabilitation, exemplified by the study conducted by Chen et al. (2022). These endeavours collectively contribute to a deeper understanding of technology acceptance within the dynamic landscape of healthcare.

The technological foundations of e-government software have stimulated the scholarly inquiry into factors influencing user acceptance. Notably, researchers such as Shyu and Huang (2011), Sipior et al. (2011), Cegarra et al. (2014) and Xie et al. (2017) have researched this domain, seeking to identify predictors of user acceptance. Conversely, Wu and Chen (2005) directed their attention toward the online tax system, while Kanak and Sogukpinar (2017) employed the Technology Acceptance Model (TAM) as a framework to investigate user acceptance of biometric authentication systems.

The rapid evolution of social media platforms has posed a challenge that necessitates a re-evaluation of their impact on traditional marketing practices. A study conducted by Lee et al. (2012) adopted the Technology Acceptance Model (TAM) to clarify the underlying mechanisms through which social media marketing influences individuals' attitudes towards Facebook event pages.

Moreover, the dynamic landscape of digital communication, marked by the rapid emergence of new platforms for information dissemination and sharing, has prompted a notable interest concerning the acceptance and adoption of social networks. This interest is evident in the research conducted by Kim (2012), Choi and Chung (2013), Lin and Kim (2016), Makki et al. (2018) and Chang and Chen (2018). The acceptance of instant messaging has also garnered scholarly attention, as exemplified by the work of Lu et al. (2009). These studies collectively contribute to our understanding of the evolving digital media landscape and the acceptance of various communication technologies.

Employing the Technology Acceptance Model (TAM) as a foundational framework, the study conducted by Hong et al. (2002) explored the impact of a range of individual variances and system characteristics on users' intention to utilize digital libraries. The investigation of digital libraries themselves is evidenced by the research conducted by Park et al. (2009) as well as Chen et al. (2016), while the utilization of information technology within library settings was examined by Sheikhshoaei and Oloumi (2011). Additionally, the interest is extended to mobile library applications, as explored by Yoon (2016), and the concept of smart libraries, as inspected by Yu and Huang (2020). These studies collectively sought to anticipate usage patterns within these technological contexts.

Besides, in the evolving technological landscape, research has probed into the acceptance of Information and Communication Technology (ICT) products for reading purposes. Specifically, investigations have been carried out regarding e-books (Jin, 2014), e-textbooks (Hsiao et al., 2015) and e-portfolios (Cheng et al., 2015; Abdullah et al., 2016) to gain insights into users' adoption behaviours. In contrast, the primary objective of the study by Liaw and Huang (2003) was to formulate and assess an individual attitude model pertaining to search engines as tools for information retrieval.

The development and evaluation of computer games have evolved in parallel with the progression of computer technology and the Internet. The history of online gaming closely mirrors the trajectory of the Internet's development, making it a focal point of several scholarly investigations. Some examples include studies on online games (Hsu & Lu, 2004), video games (Bassiouni et al., 2019), business simulation games (Tao et al., 2009), mobile social network games (Park et al., 2014; Chen et al., 2017) and emerging media entertainment technologies (Dogruel et al., 2015). These studies collectively contribute to our understanding of the dynamic landscape of digital gaming within the context of evolving technology.

Given the essential role of user acceptance in shaping the ongoing development of ICT products and services, several research endeavours have been motivated by this imperative. Particularly notable are investigations related to 3G technologies (Lopez-Nicolas et al., 2008), sensory-enabling technologies (Kim and Forsythe, 2008), digital multimedia broadcasting (Shin, 2009), Internet Protocol Television (IPTV) (Shin, 2009), decision support systems (Djamasbi et al., 2010; Mir & Padma, 2020), the online co-design process (Lee & Chang, 2011), Global Positioning System (GPS) technology (Chen & Chen, 2011), e-recruitment (Kashi and Zheng, 2013), smartphones (Joo & Sang, 2013; Rigopoulou et al., 2017), teleconferencing systems (Park et al., 2014), car navigation systems (Park & Kim, 2014; Park et al., 2015; Ge et al., 2023) and mobile navigation applications providing navigation services (Yang et al., 2021). The combined research efforts emphasize the fundamental significance of user acceptance in driving progress within a wide array of technology domains.

The latest technological advancements have introduced new possibilities into people's everyday lives, making it imperative to comprehend potential users' responses. Consequently, Technology Acceptance Model (TAM)-based models have been employed in numerous studies to assess users' acceptance of recent technologies. For instance, these models have been applied to examine haptic enabling technology (HET) (Jongchul & Sung-Joon, 2014), wearable devices (Chang et al., 2016), wearable locating systems (Kwee-Meier et al., 2016), augmented reality and wearable technologies (Guest et al., 2018), augmented reality (Li et al., 2022; Oyman et al., 2022), virtual reality (Sagnier et al., 2020) and, more recently, studies addressing smart city technology (Choi, 2022), robots based on artificial intelligence (Xu et al., 2022) and connected vehicles, which hold promise as the future of vehicular technology (Acharya & Mekker, 2022). These investigations jointly seek to illuminate the critical aspect of user acceptance in the context of emerging technologies.

In conclusion, extensive research has been conducted to assess the applicability of the Technology Acceptance Model (TAM) across a range of technologies, with authors endeavouring to identify and incorporate factors that augment the model's predictive validity. Nevertheless, the ongoing evolution of new ICT products and services, coupled with the expanding user base in terms of both quantity and diversity, presents fresh avenues for investigation. These avenues hold the potential to deepen our comprehension of technology acceptance dynamics and offer insights that could inform potential upgrades to the TAM model.

References

Abdullah, F., Ward, R., & Ahmed, E. (2016). Investigating the influence of the most commonly used external variables of TAM on students' perceived ease of use (PEOU) and perceived usefulness (PU) of e-portfolios. *Computers in Human Behavior, 63*, 75–90.

Acharya, S., & Mekker, M. (2022). Public acceptance of connected vehicles: An extension of the technology acceptance model. *Transportation Research Part F: Traffic Psychology and Behaviour, 88*, 54–68. https://doi.org/10.1016/j.trf.2022.05.002

Acikgoz, F., & Perez Vega, R. (2022). The role of privacy cynicism in consumer habits with voice assistants: A technology acceptance model perspective. *International Journal of Human–Computer Interaction, 38*(12), 1138–1152. https://doi.org/10.1080/10447318.2021.1987677

Agarwal, R., & Karahanna, E. (2000). Time flies when you're having fun: Cognitive absorption and beliefs about information technology usage. *MIS Quarterly, 24*(4), 665–694.

Ahadzadeh, A. S., Pahlevan, S. S., Ong, F. S., & Khong, K. W. (2015). Integrating health belief model and technology acceptance model: An investigation of health-related internet use. *Journal of Medical Internet Research, 17*(2), e45. https://doi.org/10.2196/jmir.3564. PMID: 25700481. PMCID: PMC4376166.

Ahmad, S., Bhatti, S. H., & Hwang, Y. (2019). E- service quality and actual use of e-banking: Explanation through the technology acceptance model. *Information Development, 36*(4), 503–519.

Ajzen, I. (1985). From intentions to actions: A theory of planned behavior. In J. Kuhl & J. Beckmann (Eds.), *Action control* (SSSP Springer series in social psychology). Springer. https://doi.org/10.1007/978-3-642-69746-3_2

Ajzen, I. (1991). The theory of planned behavior. *Organizational Behavior and Human Decision Processes, 50*(2), 179–211. https://doi.org/10.1016/0749-5978(91)90020-T

Al-Emran, M., & Granić, A. (2021). Is it still valid or outdated? A bibliometric analysis of the technology acceptance model and its applications from 2010 to 2020. In N. Al-Emran & K. Shaalan (Eds.), *Recent advances in technology acceptance models and theories* (Studies in systems, decision and control) (pp. 1–12). Springer. https://doi.org/10.1007/978-3-030-64987-6_1

Al-Emran, M., Granić, A., Al-Sharafi, M., Nisreen, A., & Sarrab, M. (2021). Examining the roles of students' beliefs and security concerns for using smartwatches in higher education. *Journal of Enterprise Information Management, 34*(4), 1229–1251. https://doi.org/10.1108/JEIM-02-2020-0052

Alexandrakis, D., Chorianopoulos, K., & Tselios, N. (2020). Older adults and Web 2.0 storytelling technologies: Probing the technology acceptance model through an age-related perspective. *International Journal of Human-Computer Interaction, 36*(17), 1–13.

Almogren, A. S. (2022). Art education lecturers' intention to continue using the blackboard during and after the COVID-19 pandemic: An empirical investigation into the UTAUT and TAM model. *Frontiers in Psychology, 13*. https://doi.org/10.3389/fpsyg.2022.944335

Almogren, A. S., & Aljammaz, N. A. (2022). The integrated social cognitive theory with the TAM model: The impact of M-learning in King Saud University art education. *Frontiers in Psychology, 13*. https://doi.org/10.3389/fpsyg.2022.1050532

Al-Rahmi, A. M., Shamsuddin, A., Alturki, U., Aldraiweesh, A., Yusof, F. M., Al-Rahmi, W. M., & Aljeraiwi, A. A. (2021). The influence of information system success and technology acceptance model on social media factors in education. *Sustainability, 13*(14), 7770–7770. https://doi.org/10.3390/su13147770

Alshare, K. A., Mesak, H. I., Grandon, E. E., & Badri, M. A. (2011). Examining the moderating role of national culture on an extended technology acceptance model. *Journal of Global Information Technology Management, 14*(3), 27–53.

Amoako-Gyampah, K. (2007). Perceived usefulness, user involvement and behavioral intention: An empirical study of ERP implementation. *Computers in Human Behavior, 23*, 1232–1248.

Amoako-Gyampah, K., & Salam, A. F. (2004). An extension of the technology acceptance model in an ERP implementation environment. *Information & Management, 41*(6), 731–745.

Arning, K., & Ziefle, M. (2007). Understanding age differences in PDA acceptance and performance. *Computers in Human Behavior, 23*(6), 2904–2927.

Baby, A., & Kannammal, A. (2020). Network path analysis for developing an enhanced TAM model: A user- centric e-learning perspective. *Computers in Human Behavior, 107*, 1–7.

Bagozzi, R. P. (1992). The self-regulation of attitudes, intentions, and behavior. *Social Psychology Quarterly, 55*(2), 178–204. Special Issue: Theoretical Advances in Social Psychology. https://www.jstor.org/stable/2786945

Bagozzi, R. P., & Warshaw, P. R. (1990). Trying to consume. *Journal of Consumer Research, 17*(2), 127–140. https://doi.org/10.1086/208543

Bandura, A. (1986). *Social foundations of thought and action: A social cognitive theory.* Prentice- Hall.

Bassiouni, D. H., Hackley, C., & Meshreki, H. (2019). The integration of video games in family-life dynamics: An adapted technology acceptance model of family intention to consume video games. *Information Technology & People, 32*(6), 1376–1396.

Beldad, A. D., & Hegner, S. M. (2018). Expanding the technology acceptance model with the inclusion of trust, social influence, and health valuation to determine the predictors of German users' willingness to continue using a fitness app: A structural equation modelling approach. *International Journal of Human-Computer Interaction, 34*(9), 882–893.

Bhattacherjee, A. (2001). Understanding information systems continuance: An expectation-confirmation model. *MIS Quarterly, 25*(3), 351–370. https://doi.org/10.1016/10.2307/3250921

Brooke, J. (1996). SUS: A "quick and dirty" usability scale. In *Usability evaluation in industry* (pp. 189–194). CRC Press.

Bueno, S., & Salmeron, J. L. (2008). TAM-based success modelling in ERP. *Interacting with Computers, 20*(6), 515–523.

Burton-Jones, A., & Hubona, G. S. (2006). The mediation of external variables in the technology acceptance model. *Information & Management, 43*, 706–717.

Calisir, F., Gumussoy, C. A., Bayraktaroglu, A. E., & Karaali, D. (2014). Predicting the intention to use a web-based learning system: Perceived content quality, anxiety, perceived system quality, image, and the technology acceptance model. *Human Factors and Ergonomics in Manufacturing & Service Industries, 24*(5), 515–531.

Castaneda, J. A., Munoz-Leiva, F., & Luque, T. (2007). Web acceptance model (WAM): Moderating effects of user experience. *Information & Management, 44*, 384–396.

Castillo-Vergara, M., Álvarez-Marín, A., Villavicencio Pinto, E., & Valdez-Juárez, L. E. (2022). Technological acceptance of industry 4.0 by students from rural areas. *Electronics, 11*(14), 2109. https://doi.org/10.3390/electronics11142109

Cegarra, J. L. M., Navarro, J. G. C., & Pachón, J. R. C. (2014). Applying the technology acceptance model to a Spanish City Hall. *International Journal of Information Management, 34*(4), 437–445.

Chan, S., & Lu, M. (2004). Understanding internet banking adoption and use behavior: A Hong Kong perspective. *Journal of Global Information Management, 12*(3), 21–43.

Chang, C.-C., & Chen, P.-Y. (2018). Analysis of critical factors for social games based on extended technology acceptance model: A DEMATEL approach. *Behaviour & Information Technology, 37*(8), 774–785.

Chang, H. S., Lee, S. C., & Ji, Y. G. (2016). Wearable device adoption model with TAM and TTF. *International Journal of Mobile Communications, 14*(5), 518–537.

Chau, P. Y. K., & Hu, P. (2002). Investigating healthcare professionals' decisions to accept telemedicine technology: An empirical test of competing theories. *Information & Management, 39*(4), 297–311.

Chen, C.-F., & Chen, P.-C. (2011). Applying the TAM to travelers' usage intentions of GPS devices. *Expert Systems with Applications, 38*(5), 6217–6221.

Chen, C.-C., & Tsai, J.-L. (2019). Determinants of behavioral intention to use the personalized location-based mobile tourism application: An empirical study by integrating TAM with ISSM. *Future Generation Computer Systems, 96*, 628–638. https://doi.org/10.1016/j.future.2017.02.028

Chen, J.-F., Chang, J.-F., Kao, C.-W., & Huang, Y.-M. (2016). Integrating ISSM into TAM to enhance digital library services: A case study of the Taiwan digital meta-library. *The Electronic Library, 34*(1), 58–73.

Chen, H., Rong, W., Ma, X., Qu, Y., & Xiong, Z. (2017). An extended technology acceptance model for mobile social gaming service popularity analysis. *Mobile Information Systems, 2017*, 1–12.

Chen, T., Chen, J., Or, C., & Lo, F. (2022). Path analysis of the roles of age, self-efficacy, and TAM constructs in the acceptance of performing upper limb exercises through immersive virtual reality games. *International Journal of Industrial Ergonomics, 91*, 103360. https://doi.org/10.1016/j.ergon.2022.103360

Cheng, S.-I., Chen, S.-C., & Yen, D. C. (2015). Continuance intention of E-portfolio system: A confirmatory and multigroup invariance analysis of technology acceptance model. *Computer Standards & Interfaces, 42*, 17–23.

Cheung, E. Y. M., & Sachs, J. (2006). Test of the technology acceptance model for a web-based information system in a Hong Kong Chinese sample. *Psychological Reports, 99*, 691–703.

Cheung, R., & Vogel, D. (2013). Predicting user acceptance of collaborative technologies: An extension of the technology acceptance model for e-learning. *Computers & Education, 63*, 160–175.

Chiu, C.-M., Lin, H.-Y., Sun, S.-Y., & Hsu, M.-H. (2009). Understanding customers' loyalty intentions towards online shopping: An integration of technology acceptance model and fairness theory. *Behaviour & Information Technology, 28*(4), 347–360.

Cho, J., Cheon, Y., Jun, J. W., & Lee, S. (2022). Digital advertising policy acceptance by out-of-home advertising firms: A combination of TAM and TOE framework. *International Journal of Advertising, 41*(3), 500–518. https://doi.org/10.1080/02650487.2021.1888562

Choi, J. (2022). Enablers and inhibitors of smart city service adoption: A dual-factor approach based on the technology acceptance model. *Telematics and Informatics, 75*, 101911. https://doi.org/10.1016/j.tele.2022.101911

Choi, G., & Chung, H. (2013). Applying the technology acceptance model to social networking sites (SNS): Impact of subjective norm and social capital on the acceptance of SNS. *International Journal of Human-Computer Interaction, 29*(10), 619–628.

Compeau, D. R., & Higgins, C. A. (1995). Computer self-efficacy: Development of a measure and initial test. *MIS Quarterly, 19*(2), 189–211.

Csikszentmihalyi, M. (1975). *Beyond boredom and anxiety: The experience of play in work and games.* San Francisco: Jossey-Bass.

Cui, Q., Hu, X., Liu, X., Zhao, L., & Wang, G. (2021). Understanding architectural designers' continuous use intention regarding BIM technology: A China case. *Buildings, 11*, 448. https://doi.org/10.3390/buildings11100448

Davis, F. D. (1986). *A technology acceptance model for empirically testing new end-user information systems: Theory and results.* Doctoral dissertation. MIT Sloan School of Management.

Davis, F. D. (1989). Perceived usefulness, perceived ease of use, and user acceptance of information technology. *MIS Quarterly, 13*(3), 319–339.

Davis, F. D., Bagozzi, R. P., & Warshaw, P. R. (1989). User acceptance of computer technology: A comparison of two theoretical models. *Management Science, 35*(8), 982–1003.

Davis, F. D., Bagozzi, R. P., & Warshaw, P. R. (1992). Extrinsic and intrinsic motivation to use computers in the workplace. *Journal of Applied Social Psychology, 22*(14), 1111–1132. https://doi.org/10.1111/j.1559-1816.1992.tb00945.x

Deci, E. L., & Ryan, R. M. (1985). *Intrinsic motivation and self-determination in human behavior.* Plenum. https://doi.org/10.1007/978-1-4899-2271-7

DeLone, W. H., & McLean, E. R. (1992). Information systems success: The quest for the dependent variable. *Information System Research, 3*(1), 60–95. https://doi.org/10.1287/isre.3.1.60

Djamasbi, S., Strong, D. M., & Dishaw, M. (2010). Affect and acceptance: Examining the effects of positive mood on the technology acceptance model. *Decision Support Systems, 48*(2), 383–394.

Dogruel, L., Joeckel, S., & Bowman, N. D. (2015). The use and acceptance of new media entertainment technology by elderly users: Development of an expanded technology acceptance model. *Behaviour & Information Technology, 34*(11), 1052–1063.

Eason, K. D. (1991). Ergonomic perspectives on advances in human-computer interaction. *Ergonomics, 34*(6), 721–741. https://doi.org/10.1080/00140139108967347

Egea, J. M. O., & González, M. V. R. (2011). Explaining physicians' acceptance of EHCR systems: An extension of TAM with trust and risk factors. *Computers in Human Behavior, 27*(1), 319–332.

Farahat, T. (2012). Applying the technology acceptance model to online learning in the Egyptian universities. *Procedia – Social and Behavioral Sciences, 64*, 95–104.

Featherman, M. S., & Pavlou, P. A. (2003). Predicting E-services adoption: A perceived risk facets perspective. *International Journal of Human-Computer Studies, 59*(4), 451–474.

Fishbein, M., & Ajzen, I. (1975). *Belief, attitude, intention and behavior: An introduction to theory and research.* Addison-Wesley.

Ge, Y., Qi, H., & Qu, W. (2023). The factors impacting the use of navigation systems: A study based on the technology acceptance model. *Transportation Research Part F: Traffic Psychology and Behaviour, 93*, 106–117. https://doi.org/10.1016/j.trf.2023.01.005

Gefen, D. (2004). What makes an ERP implementation relationship worthwhile: Linking trust mechanisms and ERP usefulness. *Journal of Management Information Systems, 21*(1), 263–288.

Gefen, D., & Straub, D. W. (1997). Gender difference in the perception and use of E-mail: An extension to the technology acceptance model. *MIS Quarterly, 21*(4), 389–400.

Gefen, D., Karahanna, E., & Straub, D. W. (2003). Trust and TAM in online shopping: An integrated model. *MIS Quarterly, 27*(1), 51–90.

Girish, V. G., Kim, M., Sharma, I., & Lee, C.-K. (2022). Examining the structural relationships among e-learning interactivity, uncertainty avoidance, and perceived risks of COVID-19: Applying extended technology acceptance model. *International Journal of Human–Computer Interaction, 38*, 742–752. https://doi.org/10.1080/10447318.2021.1970430

Goodhue, D. L., & Thompson, R. L. (1995). Task-technology fit and individual performance. *MIS Quarterly, 19*(2), 213–236. https://doi.org/10.2307/249689

Gómez-Ramirez, I., Valencia-Arias, A., & Duque, L. (2019). Approach to M-Learning acceptance among university students: An integrated model of TPB and TAM. *International Review of Research in Open and Distributed Learning, 20*(3), 141–164.

Granić, A. (2022). Educational technology adoption: A systematic review. *Education and Information Technologies, 27*, 9725–9744. https://doi.org/10.1007/s10639-022-10951-7

Granić, A. (2023). Technology adoption at individual level: Toward an integrated overview. *Universal Access in the Information Society.* https://doi.org/10.1007/s10209-023-00974-3

Gu, D., Khan, S., Khan, I. U., & Khan, S. U. (2019). Understanding mobile tourism shopping in Pakistan: An integrating framework of innovation diffusion theory and technology acceptance model. *Mobile Information Systems, 2019*, 1–18.

Guest, W., Wild, F., Vovk, A., Lefrere, P., Klemke, R., Fominykh, M., & Kuula, T. (2018). Technology acceptance model for augmented reality and wearable technologies. *Journal of Universal Computer Science, 24*(2), 192–219.

Gumussoy, C. A., Calisir, F., & Bayram, A. (2007). *Understanding the behavioral intention to use ERP systems: An extended technology acceptance model.* In 2007 IEEE International conference on industrial engineering and engineering management.

Guner, H., & Acarturk, C. (2020). The use and acceptance of ICT by senior citizens: A comparison of technology acceptance model (TAM) for elderly and young adults. *Universal Access in the Information Society, 19*, 311–330.

He, L., & Li, C. (2023). Continuance intention to use mobile learning for second language acquisition based on the technology acceptance model and self-determination theory. *Frontiers in Psychology, 14*, 1185851. https://doi.org/10.3389/fpsyg.2023.1185851

Hong, W., Thong, J. Y. L., Wong, W., & Tam, K. (2002). Determinants of user acceptance of digital libraries: An empirical examination of individual differences and system characteristics. *Journal of Management Information Systems, 18*(3), 97–124.

Horton, R. P., Buck, T., Waterson, P. E., & Clegg, C. W. (2001). Explaining intranet use with the technology acceptance model. *Journal of Information Technology, 16*(4), 237–249.

Hsiao, C.-H., Tang, K.-Y., & Lin, C.-H. (2015). Exploring college students' intention to adopt e-textbooks: A modified technology acceptance model. *Libri, 65*(2), 119–128.

Hsu, C.-L., & Lu, H.-P. (2004). Why do people play on-line games? An extended TAM with social influences and flow experience. *Information & Management, 41*(7), 853–868.

Hu, P. J., Chau, P. Y. K., Sheng, O. R. L., & Tam, K. Y. (1999). Examining the technology acceptance model using physician acceptance of telemedicine technology. *Journal of Management Information Systems, 16*(2), 91–112.

Hu, P. J., Lin, C., & Chen, H. (2005). User acceptance of intelligence and security informatics technology: A study of COPLINK. *Journal of the American Society for Information Science and Technology, 56*(3), 235–244.

Huang, L. J., Lu, M. T., & Wong, B. K. (2003). The impact of power distance on email acceptance: Evidence from the PRC. *Journal of Computer Information Systems, 44*(1), 93–101.

Huang, J.-H., Lin, Y.-R., & Chuang, S.-T. (2007). Elucidating user behavior of mobile learning: A perspective of the extended technology acceptance model. *The Electronic Library, 25*(5), 585–598.

Huang, Y.-C., Li, L.-N., Lee, H.-Y., Browning, M., & Yu, C.-P. (2023). Surfing in virtual reality: An application of extended technology acceptance model with flow theory. *Computers in Human Behavior Reports, 9,* 100252. https://doi.org/10.1016/j.chbr.2022.100252

Ifinedo, P. (2017). Examining students' intention to continue using blogs for learning: Perspectives from technology acceptance, motivational, and social-cognitive frameworks. *Computers in Human Behavior, 72,* 189–199. https://doi.org/10.1016/j.chb.2016.12.049

Jackson, C. M., Chow, S., & Leitch, R. A. (1997). Toward an understanding of the behavioral intention to use an information system. *Decision Sciences, 28*(2), 357–389.

Jin, C.-H. (2014). Adoption of e-book among college students: The perspective of an integrated TAM. *Computers in Human Behavior, 41,* 471–477.

Jongchul, O., & Sung-Joon, Y. (2014). Validation of haptic enabling technology acceptance model (HE-TAM): Integration of IDT and TAM. *Telematics and Informatics, 31*(4), 585–596.

Joo, J., & Sang, Y. (2013). Exploring Koreans' smartphone usage: An integrated model of the technology acceptance model and uses and gratifications theory. *Computers in Human Behavior, 29*(6), 2512–2518.

Kanak, A., & Sogukpinar, I. (2017). BioTAM: A technology acceptance model for biometric authentication systems. *IET Biometrics, 6*(6), 457–467.

Kashi, K., & Zheng, C. (2013). Extending technology acceptance model to the E-recruitment context in Iran. *International Journal of Selection and Assessment, 21*(1), 121–129.

Kim, S. (2012). Factors affecting the use of social software: TAM perspectives. *The Electronic Library, 30*(5), 690–706.

Kim, J., & Forsythe, S. (2008). Sensory enabling technology acceptance model (SE-TAM): A multiple-group structural model comparison. *Psychology & Marketing, 25*(9), 901–922.

Kim, S., & Garrison, G. (2009). Investigating mobile wireless technology adoption: An extension of the technology acceptance model. *Information Systems Frontiers, 11*(3), 323–333.

Kimiagari, S., & Baei, F. (2022). Promoting e-banking actual usage: Mix of technology acceptance model and technology-organisation-environment framework. *Enterprise Information Systems, 16*(8–9). https://doi.org/10.1080/17517575.2021.1894356

Kwee-Meier, S. T., Bützler, J. E., & Schlick, C. (2016). Development and validation of a technology acceptance model for safety- enhancing, wearable locating systems. *Behaviour & Information Technology, 35*(5), 394–409.

Lah, U., Lewis, J. R., & Šumak, B. (2020). Perceived usability and the modified technology acceptance model. *International Journal of Human–Computer Interaction, 36*(13), 1216–1230. https://doi.org/10.1080/10447318.2020.1727262

Lai, V. S., & Li, H. (2005). Technology acceptance model for internet banking: An invariance analysis. *Information & Management, 42*(2), 373–386.

Lederer, A. L., Maupin, D. J., Sena, M. P., & Zhuang, Y. (2000). The technology acceptance model and the world wide web. *Decision Support Systems, 29*(3), 269–282.

Lee, M.-C. (2009). Factors influencing the adoption of internet banking: An integration of TAM and TPB with perceived risk and perceived benefit. *Electronic Commerce Research and Applications, 8*(3), 130–141.

Lee, H.-H., & Chang, E. (2011). Consumer attitudes toward online mass customization: An application of extended technology acceptance model. *Journal of Computer-Mediated Communication, 16*(2), 171–200.

Lee, S., & Kim, B. (2009). Factors affecting the usage of intranet: A confirmatory study. *Computers in Human Behavior, 25*(1), 191–201.

Lee, D. Y., & Lehto, M. R. (2013). User acceptance of YouTube for procedural learning: An extension of the technology acceptance model. *Computers & Education, 61,* 193–208.

Lee, C., & Wan, G. (2010). Including subjective norm and technology trust in the technology acceptance model: A case of e-ticketing in China. *The DATA BASE for Advances in Information Systems, 41*(4), 40–51.

Lee, W., Xiong, L., & Hu, C. (2012). The effect of Facebook users' arousal and valence on intention to go to the festival: Applying an extension of the technology acceptance model. *International Journal of Hospitality Management, 31*, 819–827.

Lee, Y.-H., Hsieh, Y.-C., & Chen, Y.-H. (2013). An investigation of employees' use of e-learning systems: Applying the technology acceptance model. *Behaviour & Information Technology, 32*(2), 173–189.

Lee, J. H., Kim, J. H., & Choi, J. Y. (2019). The adoption of virtual reality devices: The technology acceptance model integrating enjoyment, social interaction, and strength of the social ties. *Telematics and Informatics, 39*, 37–48.

Leso, B. H., & Cortimiglia, M. N. (2022). The influence of user involvement in information system adoption: An extension of TAM. *Cognition, Technology & Work, 24*, 215–231. https://doi.org/10.1007/s10111-021-00685-w

Lewis, J. R., Utesch, B. S., & Maher, D. E. (2013). *UMUX-LITE: When there's no time for the SUS*. In CHI'13: Proceedings of the SIGCHI conference on human factors in computing systems (pp, 2099–2102). https://doi.org/10.1145/2470654.2481287.

Li, X.-Z., Chen, C.-C., Kang, X., & Kang, J. (2022). Research on relevant dimensions of tourism experience of intangible cultural heritage lantern festival: Integrating generic learning outcomes with the technology acceptance model. *Frontiers in Psychology, 13*, 943277. https://doi.org/10.3389/fpsyg.2022.943277

Liaw, S. S., & Huang, H. M. (2003). An investigation of user attitudes toward search engines as an information retrieval tool. *Computers in Human Behavior, 19*(6), 751–765.

Lin, C. A., & Kim, T. (2016). Predicting user response to sponsored advertising on social media via the technology acceptance model. *Computers in Human Behavior, 64*, 710–718.

Lin, P.-H., & Yeh, S.-C. (2019). How motion-control influences a vr-supported technology for mental rotation learning: From the perspectives of playfulness, gender difference and technology acceptance model. *International Journal of Human–Computer Interaction, 35*(18), 1736–1746.

Liu, K., Or, C. K., So, M., Cheung, B., Chan, B., Tiwari, A., & Tan., J. (2022). A longitudinal examination of tablet self-management technology acceptance by patients with chronic diseases: Integrating perceived hand function, perceived visual function, and perceived home space adequacy with the TAM and TPB. *Applied Ergonomics, 100*. https://doi.org/10.1016/j.apergo.2021.103667

Lopez-Nicolas, C., Molina-Castillo, F. J., & Bouwman, H. (2008). An assessment of advanced mobile services acceptance: Contributions from TAM and diffusion theory models. *Information & Management, 45*(6), 359–364.

Lu, J., Yu, C.-S., Liu, C., & Yao, J. E. (2003). Technology acceptance model for wireless Internet. *Research, 13*(3), 206–223.

Lu, Y., Zhou, T., & Wang, B. (2009). Exploring Chinese users' acceptance of instant messaging using the theory of planned behavior, the technology acceptance model, and the flow theory. *Computers in Human Behavior, 25*(1), 29–39. https://doi.org/10.1016/j.chb.2008.06.002

Lucas, H. C., & Spitler, V. K. (1999). Technology use and performance: A field study of broker workstations. *Decision Sciences, 30*(2), 291–311.

Makki, T. W., DeCook, J. R., Kadylak, T., & Lee, O. J. Y. (2018). The social value of Snapchat: An exploration of affiliation motivation, the technology acceptance model, and relational maintenance in snapchat use. *International Journal of Human–Computer Interaction, 34*(5), 410–420.

Mathieson, K., Peacock, E., & Chinn, W. C. (2001). Extending the technology acceptance model: The influence of perceived user resources. *The Data Base for Advances in Information Systems, 32*(3), 86–112.

McFarland, D. J., & Hamilton, D. (2006). Adding contextual specificity to the technology acceptance model. *Computers in Human Behavior, 22*(3), 427–447.

Melas, C. D., Zampetakis, L. A., Dimopoulou, A., & Moustakis, V. (2011). Modeling the acceptance of clinical information systems among hospital medical staff: An extended TAM model. *Journal of Biomedical Informatics, 44*, 553–564.

Mir, S. A., & Padma, T. (2020). Integrated technology acceptance model for the evaluation of agricultural decision support systems. *Journal of Global Information Technology Management, 23*(2), 138–164.

Mohammadi, H. (2015). Investigating users' perspectives on e-learning: An integration of TAM and IS success model. *Computers in Human Behavior, 45*, 359–374.

Moon, B. (1995). Paradigms in migration research: Exploring 'moorings' as a schema. *Progress in Human Geography, 19*(4), 504–524. https://doi.org/10.1177/030913259501900404

Moon, J. W., & Kim, Y. G. (2001). Extending the TAM for a world-wide- web context. *Information & Management, 38*(4), 217–230.

Moore, G. C., & Benbasat, I. (1991). Development of an instrument to measure the perceptions of adopting an information technology innovation. *Information Systems Research, 2*(3), 173–191. https://doi.org/10.1287/isre.2.3.192

Mustafa, M. H., Ahmad, M. B., Shaari, Z. H., & Jannat, T. (2021). Integration of TAM, TPB, and TSR in understanding library user behavioral utilization intention of physical vs. E-book format. *The Journal of Academic Librarianship, 47*(5), 102399. https://doi.org/10.1016/j.acalib.2021.102399

Nasri, W., & Charfeddine, L. (2012). Factors affecting the adoption of Internet banking in Tunisia: An integration theory of acceptance model and theory of planned behavior. *Journal of High Technology Management Research, 23*, 1–14.

Nayak, L. U. S., Priest, L., & White, A. P. (2010). An application of the technology acceptance model to the level of Internet usage by older adults. *Universal Access in the Information Society, 9*(4), 367–374.

Nguyen, T. T. T. (2023). Citizens' intentions to use e-government during the COVID-19 pandemic: Integrating the technology acceptance model and perceived risk theory. *Kybernetes, 52*(7), 2329–2346. https://doi.org/10.1108/K-07-2022-1023

Oliver, R. L. (1980). A cognitive model of the antecedents and consequences of satisfaction decisions. *Journal of Marketing Research, 17*(4), 460–469. https://doi.org/10.1177/002224378001700405

Ooi, K.-B., & Tan, G. W.-H. (2016). Mobile technology acceptance model: An investigation using mobile users to explore smartphone credit card. *Expert Systems with Applications, 59*(15), 33–46.

Oyman, M., Bal, D., & Ozer, S. (2022). Extending the technology acceptance model to explain how perceived augmented reality affects consumers' perceptions. *Computers in Human Behavior, 128*, 107127., ISSN 0747-5632. https://doi.org/10.1016/j.chb.2021.107127

Padilla-Meléndez, A., Aguila-Obra, A., & Garrido-Moreno, A. (2013). Perceived playfulness, gender differences and technology acceptance model in a blended learning scenario. *Computers & Education, 63*, 306–317.

Pai, F.-Y., & Huang, K.-I. (2011). Applying the technology acceptance model to the introduction of healthcare information systems. *Technological Forecasting and Social Change, 78*, 650–660.

Pal, D., & Patra, S. (2021). University students' perception of video-based learning in times of COVID-19: A TAM/TTF perspective. *International Journal of Human–Computer Interaction, 37*(10), 903–921. https://doi.org/10.1080/10447318.2020.1848164

Pan, S., & Jordan-Marsh, M. (2010). Internet use intention and adoption among Chinese older adults: From the expanded technology acceptance model perspective. *Computers in Human Behavior, 26*(5), 1111–1119.

Papakostas, C., Troussas, C., Krouska, A., & Sgouropoulou, C. (2023). Exploring users' behavioral intention to adopt mobile augmented reality in education through an extended technology acceptance model. *International Journal of Human–Computer Interaction, 39*(6), 1294–1302. https://doi.org/10.1080/10447318.2022.2062551

Parasuraman, A. (2000). Technology readiness index (TRI): A multiple-item scale to measure readiness to embrace new technologies. *Journal of Service Research, 2*, 307–320. https://doi.org/10.1177/109467050024001

Park, E., & Kim, K. J. (2013). User acceptance of long-term evolution (LTE) services An application of extended technology acceptance model. *Program: Electronic Library and Information Systems, 47*(2), 188–205.

Park, E., & Kim, K. J. (2014). An integrated adoption model of mobile cloud services: Exploration of key determinants and extension of technology acceptance model. *Telematics and Informatics, 31*(3), 376–385.

Park, E., & Kwon, S. J. (2016). The adoption of teaching assistant robots: A technology acceptance model approach. *Program-Electronic Library and Information Systems, 50*(4), 354–366.

Park, N., Roman, R., Lee, S., & Chung, J. E. (2009). User acceptance of a digital library system in developing countries: An application of the technology acceptance model. *International Journal of Information Management, 29*(3), 196–209.

Park, E., Baek, S., Ohm, J., & Chang, H. J. (2014). Determinants of player acceptance of mobile social network games: An application of extended technology acceptance model. *Telematics and Informatics, 31*(1), 3–15.

Park, E., Kim, H., & Ohm, J. Y. (2015). Understanding driver adoption of car navigation systems using the extended technology acceptance model. *Behaviour & Information Technology, 34*(7), 741–751.

Pavlou, P. A. (2003). Consumer acceptance of electronic commerce: Integrating trust and risk with the technology acceptance model. *International Journal of Electronic Commerce, 7*(3), 101–134.

Pikkarainen, T., Pikkarainen, K., Karjaluoto, H., & Pahnila, S. (2004). Consumer acceptance of online banking: An extension of the technology acceptance model. *Internet Research, 14*(3), 224–235.

Puspitasari, I., Wiambodo, A. N. R., & Soeparman, P. (2021). *The impact of expectation confirmation, technology compatibility, and customer's acceptance on e-wallet continuance intention.* In AIP Conference Proceedings 2329, 050012. https://doi.org/10.1063/5.0042269.

Razmak, J., & Bélanger, C. (2018). Using the technology acceptance model to predict patient attitude toward personal health records in regional communities. *Information Technology & People, 31*(2), 306–326.

Rebelo, F., Noriega, P., Oliveira, T., Santos, D., Carvalhais, J., & Cotrim, T. (2018). Applications and interface requirements to engage the citizens to share information in a smart city project. In F. Rebelo & M. Soares (Eds.), *Advances in ergonomics in design* (Advances in intelligent systems and computing) (Vol. 588). https://doi.org/10.1007/978-3-319-60582-1_71

Ren, L., Yang, F., Gu, C., Sun, J., & Liu, Y. (2022). A study of factors influencing Chinese college students' intention of using metaverse technology for basketball learning: Extending the technology acceptance model. *Frontiers in Psychology, 13*, 1049972. https://doi.org/10.3389/fpsyg.2022.1049972

Rigopoulou, I. D., Chaniotakis, I. E., & Kehagias, J. D. (2017). An extended technology acceptance model for predicting smartphone adoption among young consumers in Greece. *International Journal of Mobile Communications, 15*(4), 372–387.

Roberts, P., & Henderson, R. (2000). Information technology acceptance in a sample of government employees: A test of the technology acceptance model. *Interacting with Computers, 12*(5), 427–443.

Roca, J. C., Chiu, C. M., & Martinez, F. J. (2006). Understanding e-learning continuance intention: An extension of the technology acceptance model. *International Journal of Human-Computer Studies, 64*(8), 683–696. https://doi.org/10.1016/j.ijhcs.2006.01.003

Rogers, E. (1962). *Diffusion of innovations.* The Free Press.

Rogers, R. W. (1975). A protection motivation theory of fear appeals and attitude change. *Journal of Psychology, 91*(1), 93–114. https://doi.org/10.1080/00223980.1975.9915803

Rogers, E. (1995). *Diffusion of innovations* (4th ed.). The Free Press.

Saadé, R., & Bahli, B. (2005). The impact of cognitive absorption on perceived usefulness and perceived ease of use in on-line learning: An extension of the technology acceptance model. *Information & Management, 42*(2), 317–327.

Saadé, R. G., & Kira, D. (2006). The emotional state of technology acceptance. *Issues in Informing Science and Information Technology, 3*, 529–539.

Sagheer, N., Khan, K. I., Fahd, S., Mahmood, S., Rashid, T., & Jamil, H. (2022). Factors affecting adaptability of cryptocurrency: An application of technology acceptance model. *Frontiers in Psychology, 13*, 903473. https://doi.org/10.3389/fpsyg.2022.903473

Sagnier, C., Loup-Escande, E., Lourdeaux, D., Thouvenin, I., & Valléry, G. (2020). User acceptance of virtual reality: An extended technology acceptance model. *International Journal of Human-Computer Interaction, 36*(11), 1–15.

Sánchez, R. A., & Hueros, A. D. (2010). Motivational factors that influence the acceptance of Moodle using TAM. *Computers in Human Behavior, 26*(6), 1632–1640.

Sanchez-Prieto, J. C., Olmos-Miguelanez, S., & García-Penalvo, F. J. (2017). MLearning and pre-service teachers: An assessment of the behavioral intention using an expanded TAM model. *Computers in Human Behavior, 72*, 1–11.

Schepers, J., & Wetzels, M. (2007). A meta-analysis of the technology acceptance model: Investigating subjective norm and moderation effects. *Information & Management, 44*(1), 90–103.

Serenko, A. (2008). A model of user adoption of interface agents for email notification. *Interacting with Computers, 20*, 461–472.

Sharif, S. P., & Naghavi, N. (2021). Online financial trading among young adults: Integrating the theory of planned behavior, technology acceptance model, and theory of flow. *International Journal of Human–Computer Interaction, 37*(10), 949–962. https://doi.org/10.1080/1044731 8.2020.1861761

Sharma, S. K. (2019). Integrating cognitive antecedents into TAM to explain mobile banking behavioral intention: A SEM-neural network modelling. *Information Systems Frontiers, 21*, 815–827.

Sheikhshoaei, F., & Oloumi, T. (2011). Applying the technology acceptance model to Iranian engineering faculty libraries. *The Electronic Library, 29*(3), 367–378.

Shih, H. (2004). Extended technology acceptance model of internet utilization behavior. *Information & Management, 41*(6), 719–729.

Shin, D. H. (2009). Understanding user acceptance of DMB in South Korea using the modified technology acceptance model. *International Journal of Human-Computer Interaction, 25*(3), 173–198.

Shin, D.-H., & Kim, W.-Y. (2008). Applying the technology acceptance model and flow theory to Cyworld user behavior: Implication of the Web2.0 user acceptance. *Cyberpsychology & Behavior, 11*(3), 378–382.

Shyu, S. H.-P., & Huang, J.-H. (2011). Elucidating usage of e-government learning: A perspective of the extended technology acceptance model. *Government Information Quarterly, 28*(4), 491–502.

Silva, G. M., Dias, A., & Rodrigues, M. S. (2022). Continuity of use of food delivery apps: An integrated approach to the health belief model and the technology readiness and acceptance model. *Journal of Open Innovation: Technology, Market, and Complexity, 8*(3), 114. https://doi.org/10.3390/joitmc8030114

Sipior, J. C., Ward, B. T., & Connolly, R. (2011). The digital divide and t-government in the United States: Using the technology acceptance model to understand usage. *European Journal of Information Systems, 20*(3), 308–328.

Son, H., Park, Y., Kim, C., & Chou, J.-S. (2012). Toward an understanding of construction professionals' acceptance of mobile computing devices in South Korea: An extension of the technology acceptance model. *Automation in Construction, 28*, 82–90.

Spacey, R., Goulding, A., & Murray, I. (2004). Exploring the attitudes of public library staff to the internet using the TAM. *Journal of Documentation, 60*(5), 550–564.

Stern, B. B., Royne, M. B., Stafford, T. F., & Bienstock, C. C. (2008). Consumer acceptance of online auctions: An extension and revision of the TAM. *Psychology & Marketing, 25*(7), 619–636.

Svendsen, G. B., Johnsen, J.-A. K., Almås-Sørensen, L., & Vittersø, J. (2013). Personality and technology acceptance: The influence of personality factors on the core constructs of the technology acceptance model. *Behaviour & Information Technology, 32*(4), 323–334.

Tao, Y.-H., Cheng, C.-J., & Sun, S.-Y. (2009). What influences college students to continue using business simulation games? The Taiwan experience. *Computers & Education, 53*(3), 929–939.

Tavakoli, S. S., Mozaffari, A., Danaei, A., & Rashidi, E. (2023). Explaining the effect of artificial intelligence on the technology acceptance model in media: A cloud computing approach. *The Electronic Library, 41*(1), 1–29. https://doi.org/10.1108/EL-04-2022-0094

Taylor, S., & Todd, P. A. (1995a). Understanding information technology usage: A test of competing models. *Information Systems Research, 6*(2), 144–176. https://doi.org/10.1287/isre.6.2.144

Taylor, S., & Todd, P. A. (1995b). Assessing IT usage: The role of prior experience. *MIS Quarterly, 19*(4), 561–570. https://doi.org/249633

Thompson, R. L., Higgins, C. A., & Howell, J. M. (1991). Personal computing: Toward a conceptual model of utilization. *MIS Quarterly, 15*(1), 124–143. https://doi.org/10.2307/249443

Tornatzky, L., & Fleischer, M. (1990). *The process of technology innovation.* Lexington Books.

Travers, J. (2015). *Uses and gratifications of wearable technology adoption.* Thesis at University of Missouri. https://mospace.umsystem.edu/xmlui/handle/10355/58517

Triandis, H. C. (1980). *Values, attitudes, and interpersonal behavior.* In Nebraska symposium on motivation, 1979: Beliefs, attitudes, and values (pp. 195–259). University of Nebraska Press.

Tung, F.-C., Lee, M. S., Chen, C.-C., & Hsu, Y.-S. (2009). An extension of financial cost and TAM model with IDT for exploring users' behavioral intentions to use the CRM information system. *Social Behavior and Personality, 37*(5), 621–626.

Tzou, R.-C., & Lu, H.-P. (2009). Exploring the emotional, aesthetic, and ergonomic facets of innovative product on fashion technology acceptance model. *Behaviour & Information Technology, 28*(4), 311–322.

van der Heijden, H. (2004). User acceptance of hedonic information systems. *MIS Quarterly, 28*(4), 695–704.

Venkatesh, V. (2000). Determinants of perceived ease of use: Integrating control, intrinsic motivation, and emotion into the technology acceptance model. *Information Systems Research, 11*(4), 342–365.

Venkatesh, V., & Bala, H. (2008). Technology acceptance model 3 and a research agenda on interventions. *Decision Sciences, 29*(2), 273–315.

Venkatesh, V., & Davis, F. D. (2000). A theoretical extension of the technology acceptance model: Four longitudinal field studies. *Management Science, 46*(2), 186–204.

Venkatesh, V., & Morris, M. G. (2000). Why don't men ever stop to ask for directions? Gender, social influence, and their role in technology acceptance and usage behavior. *MIS Quarterly, 24*(1), 115–139.

Venkatesh, V., Morris, M. G., Davis, G. B., & Davis, F. D. (2003). User acceptance of information technology: Towards a unified view. *MIS Quarterly, 27*(3), 425–478. https://www.jstor.org/stable/30036540

Venkatesh, V., Thong, J. Y. L., & Xu, X. (2016). Unified theory of acceptance and use of technology: A synthesis and the road ahead. *Journal of the Association for Information Systems, 17*(5), 328–376. https://ssrn.com/abstract=2800121

Vijayasarathy, L. R. (2004). Predicting consumer intentions to use on-line shopping: The case for an augmented technology acceptance model. *Information & Management, 41*(6), 747–762.

Wang, G., & Shin, C. (2022). Influencing factors of usage intention of Metaverse education application platform: Empirical evidence based on PPM and TAM models. *Sustainability, 14*, 17037. https://doi.org/10.3390/su142417037

Wang, C., Cui, W., Zhang, Y., & Shen, H. (2022a). Exploring short video apps users' travel behavior intention: Empirical analysis based on SVA-TAM model. *Frontiers in Psychology, 13*, 912177. https://doi.org/10.3389/fpsyg.2022.912177

Wang, Y.- M., Wei, C.- L., & Wang, M.- W. (2022b), Factors influencing students' adoption intention of brain–computer interfaces in a game-learning context. *Library Hi Tech*, Ahead-of-print No. ahead-of-print. https://doi.org/10.1108/LHT-12-2021-0506.

Wei, Y., Wang, C., Zhu, S., Xue, H., & Chen, F. (2018). Online purchase intention of fruits: Antecedents in an integrated model based on technology acceptance model and perceived risk theory. *Frontiers in Psychology, 9*, 1521. https://doi.org/10.3389/fpsyg.2018.01521

Won, D., Chiu, W., & Byun, H. (2023). Factors influencing consumer use of a sport-branded app: The technology acceptance model integrating app quality and perceived enjoyment. *Asia Pacific Journal of Marketing and Logistics, 35*(5), 1112–1133. https://doi.org/10.1108/APJML-09-2021-0709

Wu, I.-L., & Chen, J.-L. (2005). An extension of trust and TAM model with TPB in the initial adoption of on-line tax: An empirical study. *International Journal of Human-Computer Studies, 62*(6), 784–808.

Wu, B., & Chen, X. (2017). Continuance intention to use MOOCs: Integrating the technology acceptance model (TAM) and task technology fit (TTF) model. *Computers in Human Behavior, 67*, 1–12.

Wu, J., & Song, S. (2021). Older adults' online shopping continuance intentions: Applying the technology acceptance model and the theory of planned behavior. *International Journal of Human–Computer Interaction, 37*(10), 938–948. https://doi.org/10.1080/10447318.2020.1861419

Wu, J.-H., & Wang, S.-C. (2005). What drives mobile commerce? An empirical evaluation of the revised technology acceptance model. *Information & Management, 42*(5), 719–729.

Wu, C.-S., Cheng, F.-F., Yen, D. C., & Huang, Y.-W. (2011a). User acceptance of wireless technology in organizations: A comparison of alternative models. *Computer Standards & Interfaces, 33*, 50–58.

Wu, K., Zhao, Y., Zhu, Q., Tan, X., & Zheng, H. (2011b). A meta-analysis of the impact of trust on technology acceptance model: Investigation of moderating influence of subject and context type. *International Journal of Information Management, 31*(6), 572–581.

Xie, Q., Song, W., & Peng, X. (2017). Predictors for e-government adoption: Integrating TAM, TPB, trust and perceived risk. *The Electronic Library, 1*, 2–20.

Xu, N., Wang, K. J., & Lin, C. Y. (2022). Technology acceptance model for lawyer robots with AI: A quantitative survey. *International Journal of Social Robotics, 14*, 1043–1055. https://doi.org/10.1007/s12369-021-00850-1

Yang, H., & Yoo, Y. (2004). It's all about attitude: Revisiting the technology acceptance model. *Decision Support Systems, 38*(1), 19–31.

Yang, L., Bian, Y., Zhao, X., Liu, X., & Yao, X. (2021). Drivers' acceptance of mobile navigation applications: An extended technology acceptance model considering drivers' sense of direction, navigation application affinity and distraction perception. *International Journal of Human-Computer Studies, 145*, 102507. https://doi.org/10.1016/j.ijhcs.2020.102507

Yen, D. C., Wu, C.-S., Cheng, F.-F., & Huang, Y.-W. (2010). Determinants of users' intention to adopt wireless technology: An empirical study by integrating TTF with TAM. *Computers in Human Behavior, 26*(5), 906–915. https://doi.org/10.1016/j.chb.2010.02.005

Yi, M. Y., & Hwang, Y. (2004). Predicting the use of web-based information systems: Self-efficacy, enjoyment, learning goal orientation, and the technology acceptance model. *International Journal of Human-Computer Studies, 59*(4), 431–449.

Yin, L. X., & Lin, H. C. (2022). Predictors of customers' continuance intention of mobile banking from the perspective of the interactivity theory. *Economic Research/EkonomskaIstraživanja, 35*(1), 6820–6849. https://doi.org/10.1080/1331677X.2022.2053782

Yoon, H.-Y. (2016). User acceptance of mobile library applications in academic libraries: An application of the technology acceptance model. *The Journal of Academic Librarianship, 42*(6), 687–693.

Yoon, C. (2018). Extending the TAM for green IT: A normative perspective. *Computers in Human Behavior, 83*, 129–139.

Yoon, C., & Kim, S. (2007). Convenience and TAM in a ubiquitous computing environment: The case of wireless LAN. *Electronic Commerce Research and Applications, 6*(1), 102–112.

Yousafzai, S. Y., Foxall, G. R., & Pallister, J. G. (2010). Explaining internet banking behavior: Theory of reasoned action, theory of planned behavior, or technology acceptance model? *Journal of Applied Social Psychology, 40*(5), 1172–1202.

Yu, X. (2022). Farmers' trust in government and participation intention toward rural tourism through TAM: The moderation effect of perceived risk. *Frontiers in Psychology, 13*, 1023280. https://doi.org/10.3389/fpsyg.2022.1023280

Yu, K., & Huang, G. (2020). Exploring consumers' intent to use smart libraries with technology acceptance model. *The Electronic Library, 38*(3), 447–461. https://doi.org/10.1108/EL-08-2019-0188

Yu, J., Ha, I., Choi, M., & Rho, J. (2005). Extending the TAM for a t-commerce. *Information & Management, 42*(7), 965–976.

Zainab, B., Awais Bhatti, M., & Alshagawi, M. (2017). Factors affecting e-training adoption: An examination of perceived cost, computer self-efficacy and the technology acceptance model. *Behaviour & Information Technology, 36*(12), 1261–1273.

Zhang, S., Zhao, J., & Tan, W. (2008). Extending TAM for online learning systems: An intrinsic motivation perspective. *Tsinghua Science and Technology, 13*(3), 312–317.

Zhang, T., Shen, S., Zheng, S., Liu, Z., Qu, X., & Tao, D. (2020). Predicting unsafe behaviors at nuclear power plants: An integration of theory of planned behavior and technology acceptance model. *International Journal of Industrial Ergonomics, 80*, 103047. https://doi.org/10.1016/j.ergon.2020.103047

Zobeidi, T., Homayoon, S. B., Yazdanpanah, M., Komendantova, N., & Warner, L. A. (2023). Employing the TAM in predicting the use of online learning during and beyond the COVID-19 pandemic. *Frontiers in Psychology, 14*, 1104653. https://doi.org/10.3389/fpsyg.2023.1104653

Chapter 3
Revolution of TAM

Abstract The chapter conducts an in-depth investigation of the Technology Acceptance Model (TAM) through a comprehensive systematic review, offering profound insights into the TAM universe. Utilizing a concept-centric methodology, strict search criteria and parameters controlling the inclusion of representative body of evidence, this examination encompasses both a meta-review of TAM and a narrative review of primary studies. Classifying 23 emerged TAM-focused reviews and meta-analyses based on their investigative focus, the chapter examines studies on the core model, those exploring novel variables within TAM and reviews targeting diverse applications across contexts. Chronologically exploring and categorizing 127 primary studies within the landscape of TAM research, it discerns patterns across geographical and technological dimensions, offering a detailed understanding of the model's extension and application. Synthesizing significant findings from analysed primary studies, the chapter provides a comprehensive analysis of various variables predicting all core constructs of TAM, including the determinants of its two key drivers of user acceptance — perceived usefulness and perceived ease of use. This extensive exploration contributes to the ongoing revolution of TAM, solidifying its status as a leading established theory and a parsimonious yet powerful model for explaining, predicting and enhancing user acceptance in diverse technological deployments.

Keywords Systematic review · Meta-review · Narrative review · Technology Acceptance Model · TAM · TAM universe

3.1 Methodology for Conducting a Systematic Review

In addition to a meta-review encompassing recognized TAM-related reviews and meta-analyses, this chapter introduces a narrative review of TAM primary studies, forming the foundational landscape of TAM research (cf. Siddaway et al., 2019). This comprehensive approach enhances the credibility of the review's conclusions and recommendations, ensuring they are grounded in the most representative and relevant body of evidence available.

The review employs a concept-centric methodology, focusing on specific topics to structure its analytical framework, allowing for a more in-depth and focused investigation. This approach avoids being confined to a selection of mainstream journals or conferences within a delimited time frame (Webster & Watson, 2002). Such an approach minimizes potential subjectivity in findings attributable to temporal trends or journal preferences. Notably, research trajectories evolve over time, leading to varying prominence of specific research methodologies. Additionally, certain journals might cultivate a predisposition towards particular research approaches (Hrastinski, 2008).

The overarching aim is to systematically identify, evaluate and analyse the available academic literature concerning the Technology Acceptance Model (TAM), with the intention of achieving the following objectives:

- Categorize TAM reviews and meta-analyses based on their investigative focus, including the examination of the core model, exploration of novel variables within TAM and the diverse applications of TAM across contexts.
- Chronologically explore and categorize TAM primary studies within the foundational landscape of TAM research, discerning patterns across geographical and technological dimensions for a comprehensive understanding of the model's evolution and application.
- Categorize and synthesize main findings from analysed primary studies, providing a comprehensive understanding of TAM's core constructs, including the two key determinants of user acceptance — perceived usefulness and perceived ease of use.

The adopted approach adhered to the systematic review framework proposed by Kitchenham (2004). A methodical three-step guideline was employed, covering the phases of planning, execution and documentation. It is important to emphasize that the publications chosen through this methodological review are intentionally non-exhaustive, serving as a lens to examine evolving themes within this research trajectory over the preceding three decades.

During the planning phase, a preliminary assessment of the existing literature identified publications with potential relevance. Given the extensive body of work by global researchers in the domain of technology acceptance and adoption, it is important to note that the scope of this review could not be all-encompassing. Instead, it focused on contributions that can serve as representatives of the field.

The primary objective of the preliminary assessment was to formulate an effective search strategy and identify pertinent electronic repositories to explore. Through a series of trial searches involving diverse combinations of search terms derived from the research objectives, we defined the subsequent search query (keywords) that encapsulates the scope and diversity inherent in the field:

(TAM OR "Technology Acceptance Model")
Moreover, the identification of the targeted resources was undertaken. Given the extensive global research efforts, a series of preliminary searches were conducted within the Web of Science (WoS) database in July 2023. The aim of these searches

Table 3.1 Search terms and outcomes within the Web of Science (WoS) database (July 2023)

Search string (TAM OR "Technology Acceptance Model")		
Selected database	Search field	Search results
WoS – All Databases	Topic	40.233
WoS – All Databases	Title	5.100
WoS – Core Collection (CC)	Topic	23.779
WoS – Core Collection (CC)	Title	3.106
WoS – Current Contents Connect (CCC)	Topic	13.282
WoS – Current Contents Connect (CCC)	Title	1.323

was to identify an additional filter for refining the search process (see Table 3.1). As indicated in the table, a substantial volume of search outcomes was yielded across the majority of chosen databases and search parameters.

Consequently, the decision was made to emphasize peer-reviewed journal articles, ensuring the inclusion of studies that have undergone rigorous evaluation and meet academic standards. To achieve this, the Current Contents Connect (CCC) database, renowned for providing complete tables of contents and bibliographic information from the world's esteemed scholarly journals, was systematically queried. Additionally, this database was searched for journal publications containing specific keywords within their titles.

Finally, the establishment of clear and well-structured criteria for inclusion and exclusion stands as a matter of utmost significance when undertaking a systematic review. These criteria act as a filter, allowing inclusion only for those studies that substantiate the comprehension and progression of the Technology Acceptance Model.

By precisely delineating the characteristics necessary for a study's eligibility, we ensured that the selected publications closely align with the overarching objective of the review. Consequently, the parameters controlling the inclusion of studies encapsulated the following facets:

– Adherence to the core TAM: studies selected for inclusion shall adhere to the foundational principles of the Technology Acceptance Model, thereby upholding the integrity and conceptual framework of TAM; this criterion ensures the inclusion of studies that uphold the essence of TAM's theoretical underpinnings.
– Original peer-reviewed research in English: inclusion shall be reserved for studies that offer original scholarly insights and have undergone rigorous peer-reviewed evaluation; the demand of English-language publications assures the accessibility and comprehensibility of the selected studies within the academic community.

Moreover, it is imperative to predefine the exclusion criteria with precision in order to uphold transparency and replicability throughout the course of the review. As such, the ensuing exclusion criteria were embraced for a TAM-focused systematic review:

– Duplicate studies: duplicate studies that have been identified through the search process shall be excluded; this criterion helps to avoid bias and redundancy in the review.
– Topic relevance: studies that do not directly address the Technology Acceptance Model as a core model shall be excluded; this criterion ensures that the included studies are directly relevant to TAM-focused review.
– Quality assessment: studies that do not meet predetermined study design criteria shall be excluded; this criterion allows to prioritize studies with robust methodologies, appropriate sample sizes, and adequate reporting of results.

Extensive scholarly endeavours have been directed towards the exploration of the Technology Acceptance Model from different perspectives. Undertaking a comprehensive review would have been challenging without the careful imposition of specific search criteria. It is essential to acknowledge that the selected review protocol does carry a drawback — certain valuable publications might not have been included within its scope. For instance, Chuttur (2009) presents a synthesis of the TAM's evolution, key applications, extensions, constraints and critical examinations, drawing from a selective list of published works. However, it is noteworthy that the journal wherein this work is published does not find representation within the Current Contents Connect (CCC) database.

3.2 Meta-review of TAM-focused Reviews and Meta-analyses

3.2.1 Conducting the Meta-review

For the purpose of this meta-review, a literature search was undertaken in July 2023, employing a defined search string ("TAM" OR "Technology Acceptance Model"). The Current Contents Connect (CCC) database served as the primary resource for this search, and no temporal restrictions were imposed. In total, 77 review articles written in the English language, containing the terms "TAM" or "Technology Acceptance Model" within their publication titles, were identified.

With the dual objective of maximizing the retrieval of pertinent reviews and meta-analyses, while also taking into account domains characterized by extensive research on the Technology Acceptance Model, the search results were refined within eight distinct Research Areas:

– Behavioural Sciences
– Computer Science
– Psychology
– Information Science, Library Science
– Business Economics
– Communication
– Education, Educational Research
– Engineering

The obtained list of 27 review articles underwent a thorough examination of titles and abstracts to ascertain alignment with the established inclusion criteria. During this analysis, it was identified that two publications were duplicates, and three were subsequently excluded due to their divergence from the subject of technology acceptance. These exclusions were necessary as the term "TAM" was employed in contexts such as referencing the cave phenomenon in northern Laos, rather than the intended concept of technology acceptance.

The qualified academic literature meeting the specified criteria was retained, resulting in a total of 22 peer-reviewed journal publications with unique titles for subsequent analysis. Comprehensive reading and summarization of the complete texts of these selected publications followed. Of this selection, 13 publications were omitted as they met one or more of the aforementioned exclusion criteria, resulting in a final count of 9 filtered review articles.

Moreover, an additional collection of 14 TAM-related meta-analyses, reviews and systematic reviews, sourced and gathered by the authors themselves, was included. These entries comprise journal publications recognized by the authors, albeit not conforming to the initial screening criteria. Consequently, a comprehensive assessment and analysis encompassing a total of 23 reviews and meta-analyses on the Technology Acceptance Model have been undertaken. This meta-review, by its very nature, presents a comprehensive and illustrative account, underscoring the expansive adoption and utilization of the TAM framework.

The flow diagram showed in Fig. 3.1 offers a visual representation of the sequential stages involved in the conducted process of literature selection.

3.2.2 Results of the Meta-review

A total of 23 extensive literature reviews and meta-analyses concerning the Technology Acceptance Model (TAM) have emerged as a result of the completed meta-review. These publications are categorized into three distinct groups based on their investigative focus:

- Reviews and meta-analytical studies focused on the TAM as the core investigatory model
- Reviews and meta-analytical studies centred around novel variables, or distinct facets within the TAM framework
- Reviews and meta-analyses pertaining to applications of the TAM across various contexts

Figure 3.2 shows a visual representation of the chronological progression of the three categories, highlighting significant years and applicable publications for each group with a specific investigatory focus.

An overview of the identified literature reviews and meta-analyses pertaining to the Technology Acceptance Model (TAM) is presented in Table 3.2. In addition to providing fundamental details about the chosen publications, such as author(s),

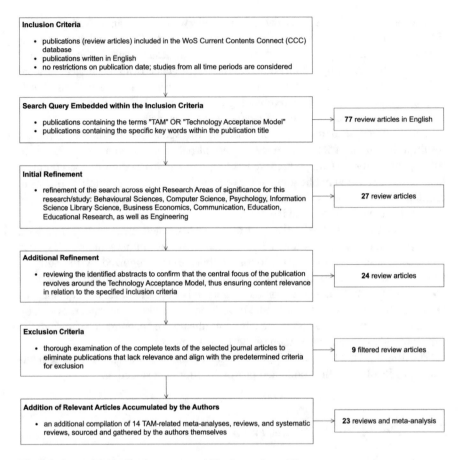

Fig. 3.1 Stages of the selection process within the conducted literature meta-review

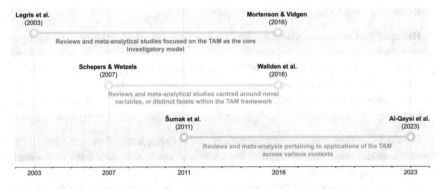

Fig. 3.2 Chronological evolution of identified categories in TAM reviews and meta-analyses

Table 3.2 Three categories of identified reviews and meta-analyses

Author(s) and pub-year	Journal	Review method	Number of studies	Field/Technology
Reviews and meta-analytical studies focused on the TAM as the core investigatory model				
Mortenson and Vidgen (2016)	Int. Journal of Information Management	Computational literature review	3.386 articles	TAM articles
Marangunić and Granić (2015)	Universal Access in the Information Society	Systematic literature review	85 publications	TAM articles
Turner et al. (2010)	Information and Software Technology	Systematic literature review	79 empirical studies	TAM articles
King and He (2006)	Information & Management	Statistical meta-analysis	88 studies	TAM articles
Legris et al. (2003)	Information & Management	Meta-analysis	22 articles	TAM articles
Reviews and meta-analytical studies centred around novel variables, or distinct facets within the TAM framework				
Walldén et al. (2016)	Universal Access in the Information Society	Literature review	24 studies	Objective measurement
Wu and Du (2012)	European Journal of Information Systems	Meta-analysis	189 articles	BI and usage constructs
Wu et al. (2011)	Int. Journal of Information Management	Meta-analysis	128 articles	Trust in technology
Wu and Lederer (2009)	MIS Quarterly	Meta-analysis	71 empirical studies	Voluntariness
Schepers and Wetzels (2007)	Information & Management	Quantitative meta-analysis	63 empirical studies	Subjective norm
Reviews and meta-analyses pertaining to applications of the TAM across various contexts				
Granić and Marangunić (2019)	British Journal of Educational Technology	Systematic literature review	71 studies	TAM in educational context
Yu (2020)	Journal of Information Technology Research	Co-citation analysis	205 scientific papers	TAM in educational context
Al-Qaysi et al. (2023)	Technology in Society	Systematic literature review	45 studies	TAM in educational context / adoption of social media
Scherer et al. (2019)	Computers & Education	Meta-analysis	114 empirical studies	TAM in educational context / teacher adoption of technology
Al-Emran et al. (2018)	Computers & Education	Systematic literature review	87 articles	TAM in educational context / m-learning

(continued)

Table 3.2 (continued)

Author(s) and pub-year	Journal	Review method	Number of studies	Field/Technology
Šumak et al. (2011)	Computers in Human Behaviour	Meta-analysis	42 studies	TAM in educational context/e-learning
Tao et al. (2020)	Computers in Human Behaviour	Meta-analysis	67 studies	TAM for health information technologies
Chauhan and Jaiswal (2017)	Journal of Enterprise Information Management	Statistical meta-analysis	111 studies	TAM in health care context
Al-Qaysi et al. (2020)	Education and Information Technologies	Systematic literature review	57 research articles	TAM in social media context
Santini et al. (2019)	Behaviour & Information Technology	Systematic literature review	142 studies	TAM for banking sector
Wang and Goh (2017)	Cyberpsychology, Behaviour and Social Networking	Meta-analysis	50 articles	TAM for video games
Šumak et al. (2017)	Computer Science and Information Systems	Systematic literature review	89 papers	TAM for e-business
Ingham et al. (2015)	Information & Management	Qualitative and meta-analytic review	109 studies	TAM for e-shopping

publication year and journal, the table provides insights into the employed review methodologies, the quantity of studies under examination and the relevant application fields or technologies considered. The systematic classification of TAM reviews and meta-analyses based on investigatory focus, along with the emphasized key findings of the conducted study, is presented in the subsequent text.

(a) *Reviews and Meta-analytical Studies Focused on the TAM as the Core Investigatory Model*

Legris et al. (2003) disseminated an assessment of empirical investigations employing both TAM and TAM2, revealing a measure of inconsistency and ambiguity in the findings. The authors posited that these inconsistencies may indicate the omission of significant factors within both models. As a corollary, it was deduced that while TAM maintains its usefulness, its potential for predictive accuracy necessitates augmentation through integration within a more expansive theoretical framework. Furthermore, the authors offered the recommendation that TAM's refinement should encompass the incorporation of organizational and social determinants.

King and He (2006) conducted a quantitative meta-analysis encompassing the application of the Technology Acceptance Model (TAM) across diverse domains. The outcomes underscored the potency and robustness of TAM as a theoretical model. Notably, the measures inherent to TAM exhibited a high degree of reliability, rendering them applicable across an array of contextual settings, thereby implying its broad-reaching prospective utility. Furthermore, the model was identified as a "complete mediating" framework, signifying that the impact of ease of use on behavioural intention is predominantly channelled through the intermediary factor of usefulness.

Turner et al. (2010) conducted a systematic literature review aimed at investigating the capacity of the Technology Acceptance Model (TAM) to anticipate actual usage, employing both subjective and objective metrics of practical usage. Their endeavour builds upon the precedent review by Legris et al. (2003), which explored the association between TAM variables and actual usage patterns. The authors concluded that exercising carefulness is imperative when applying the Model beyond the confines of its validated context. Their research findings illuminated that the TAM's core constructs, namely perceived ease of use and perceived usefulness, may not exhibit a substantial propensity to accurately predict the actual usage of technology, as compared to predictive power of behavioural intention.

In their systematic review of the literature, Marangunić and Granić (2015) meticulously examined and categorized chosen publications aligned with the Technology Acceptance Model (TAM), delineating their focal points into three distinct categories: TAM literature reviews, the evolution and expansion of TAM and the modifications and applications of TAM, as explicitly articulated by the authors of the respective publications. The comprehensive review underscored an ongoing progress in the identification of novel factors possessing substantial influence over the core constructs of the Model. However, given that several unexplored realms of potential application remain unexploited, the analysis identified a number of prospective avenues warranting future research endeavours.

Mortenson and Vidgen (2016) employed a computational literature review (CLR) technique within the context of the Technology Acceptance Model, presenting CLR as a potential complementary part to a broader literature review procedure. The authors opted to illustrate the CLR approach through the lens of the Model for several reasons. Primarily, the Technology Acceptance Model (TAM) occupies a central position in the landscape of information system research, enjoying widespread application across numerous domains. Additionally, the extensive body of TAM-related literature presents a considerable challenge for manual interpretation, thereby necessitating the assistance of computational tools.

(b) *Reviews and Meta-analytical Studies Centred Around Novel Variables, or Distinct Facets Within the TAM Framework*

Schepers and Wetzels (2007) embarked on a quantitative meta-analysis encompassing previous research concerning the Technology Acceptance Model (TAM), with the overarching aim of deriving substantiated conclusions pertaining to the significance of the subjective norm. Additionally, they undertook a comparative analysis of TAM results, factoring in the moderating influences of three distinct categories: an individual-related factor (respondent type), a technology-related factor (technology category) and a contingent factor (cultural context). The findings indicated a significant influence of the subjective norm on both perceived usefulness and the behavioural intention to use technology. Notably, the outcomes also illuminated the presence of moderating effects across all three aforementioned categories.

The conducted meta-analysis by Wu and Lederer (2009) has delivered substantial affirmation for the hypotheses positing that voluntariness, contingent upon the environmental context, moderates the effects of the ease of use and usefulness on behavioural intention. However, the effect of ease of use on usefulness remains unaltered by the presence of environment-based voluntariness. This investigation not only contributes to delineating the distinction between user-based and environment-based voluntariness but also enhances the overall comprehension of user acceptance pertaining to information technology within varying system-use environments.

Wu et al. (2011) executed a meta-analytical investigation, drawing from a corpus of preceding studies rooted in the Technology Acceptance Model (TAM), with the principal objective of substantiating assertions concerning the pivotal role of trust. Additionally, the study examined chosen TAM studies by considering the moderating effects related to the subject's classification (students or non-students) and the contextual categorization (commercial or non-commercial). The outcomes substantiated the noteworthy impact of trust on the variables inherent to TAM.

Wu and Du (2012) conducted a comprehensive critical assessment and comparative analysis of the core constructs of the Technology Acceptance Model (TAM), along with their interrelations with critical determinants of technology acceptance. The outcomes of their investigation unveiled that existing research models predicting behavioural intention may not predict system usage. It was also concluded that behavioural intention is not a suitable surrogate for actual usage and that major research attention should be given to usage rather than to behavioural intention. Lastly, within the spectrum of three usage constructs (reported, actual and assessed), assessed usage exhibits the highest correlation with behavioural intention, while actual usage displays the weakest relationship with behavioural intention.

Given the infrequent utilization of objective measurements within the Technology Acceptance Model (TAM) framework, Walldén et al. (2016) undertook an examination of user acceptance studies employing TAM in conjunction with objective usage measurements. In this study, the authors documented instances within TAM-focused research where objective usage measurements were integrated and contemplated the methodologies employed for capturing these objective measures. Recognizing the idea of objective measurement as signifying the utilization of system-generated or externally derived data (external actor records the usage), the outcomes revealed that a substantial proportion of the analysed articles predominantly relied on log data automatically gathered by the system itself.

(c) *Reviews and Meta-analyses Pertaining to Applications of the TAM across Various Contexts*

A notable majority of the identified reviews, exploring the application of the Technology Acceptance Model (TAM) across a range of domains, centred primarily on the educational sphere. More precisely, among the 13 journal publications that were uncovered, 6 of them were dedicated to an in-depth exploration of TAM's applicability within educational contexts. This encompassed a comprehensive examination of TAM's role in educational settings at large, as seen in two studies (Yu, 2020) and (Granić & Marangunić, 2019). The remaining studies within this cluster focused with greater specificity on various educational dimensions, such as the adoption of e-learning (Šumak et al., 2011) and m-learning (Al-Emran et al., 2018), technology adoption among educators (Scherer et al., 2019) and the adoption of social media within educational environments (Al-Qaysi et al., 2023).

Moreover, a couple of investigations ventured into the healthcare domain, further broadening the scope, specifically (Tao et al., 2020) and (Chauhan & Jaiswal, 2017). Beyond this, the remaining studies traversed a diverse spectrum of areas, encompassing the domain of social media (Al-Qaysi et al., 2020), the banking sector (Santini et al., 2019), the video game domain (Wang & Goh, 2017), the e-business sector (Šumak et al., 2017 and the landscape of e-shopping (Ingham et al., 2015).

The systematic literature review conducted by Granić and Marangunić (2019) provided a thorough and evaluative survey of the present landscape of research endeavours concerning the acceptance of the Technology Acceptance Model (TAM) within the domain of learning and teaching. This encompassed a wide spectrum of learning domains, learning technologies and user profiles. The primary outcomes of this review underscored the credibility of TAM, along with its various versions, in serving as a robust framework for evaluating an array of learning technologies. In a general sense, the core constructs of TAM, namely perceived ease of use and perceived usefulness, were established as antecedent factors significantly influencing the adoption and acceptance of technology-assisted learning.

Carried out by Yu (2020), the study undertook an analysis of the co-citations pertaining to the TAM within the realm of education. This analysis encompassed both the core TAM and its various extended versions. The investigation delved into the co-citational occurrences surrounding TAM, expounding upon aspects such as citation frequencies, bursts, betweenness centrality and sigma values. Additionally, the study encompassed an examination of the fundamental conceptual underpinnings that constitute user acceptance models.

While Al-Qaysi et al. (2020) conducted a review to shed light on the utilization of social media within higher education through the lens of the Technology Acceptance Model (TAM), a recent systematic literature review by Al-Qaysi Granić et al. (2023) approached the TAM from alternate perspectives. Specifically, their study delved into the identification of factors influencing the adoption of social media in an educational context and contributed a coherent taxonomy to serve as a guiding framework for subsequent research. These influential factors were categorized into three distinct groupings, encompassing external factors, antecedents of behavioural intention and moderating factors. The findings of their study highlighted that perceived enjoyment, subjective norm, social influence, self-efficacy, perceived critical mass and perceived trust emerged as the most frequently integrated external factors augmenting the original TAM. Moreover, the antecedents of behavioural intention were organized into three distinct clusters, corresponding to user-related, social and technological dimensions. In terms of moderating factors, perceived enjoyment emerged as a predominant factor in several analysed studies, followed by flow experience, hedonic attitude, utilitarian attitude, impulsiveness, media experience and media richness. A notable observation from the main findings pertained to the demographic aspect of the data collection, as the majority of studies under examination predominantly gathered data from students enrolled in the business discipline. Furthermore, Facebook emerged as the primary application commonly employed for educational purposes across the majority of the inspected studies.

The main findings stemming from the research on TAM with regard to mobile learning (m-learning), as investigated by Al-Emran et al. (2018), underline that a significant portion of TAM studies related to m-learning have primarily concentrated on the augmentation of TAM through the inclusion of external variables. Subsequently, a lesser but noteworthy portion of studies has expanded the TAM framework by incorporating factors from other theories or models. The majority of the analysed studies have been carried out within higher education environments, with a particular emphasis on assessing the acceptance of m-learning within student populations. Moreover, the prevalent focus of these studies has been observed within the humanities and educational domains, followed by the information technology and computer science, among other contextual domains.

Šumak et al. (2011) undertook a comprehensive meta-analysis of the causal effect magnitudes characterizing the interrelationships within the Technology Acceptance Model (TAM). The analysis brought to light that TAM occupies a pre-eminent position as the most widely employed theory of acceptance within the realm of e-learning adoption investigation. Moreover, the study showed that the extent of the causal effects among distinct TAM-related factors manifests variances contingent upon the user type and the particular e-learning technology under examination. The findings revealed that the perceived ease of use and the perceived usefulness exhibit a consistent influence upon user attitudes towards the use of e-learning technology, regardless of user demographics and the specific context of e-learning technology deployment.

Despite the prevailing consensus regarding the predictive factors within TAM that pertain to teachers' technology adoption, the endeavour undertaken by Scherer et al. (2019) involved a meta-analysis coupled with structural equation modelling approaches to elucidate specific aspects of concern. This approach aimed to provide greater clarity to certain intricacies. The meta-analytical findings substantiate the TAM's pertinence when applied to samples of educators, thereby clarifying certain inconsistencies observed within the model's relationships. This includes the identification of direct influences exerted by the TAM's core constructs upon both technology use and usage intentions. Overall, the study underscores the robustness of TAM as a conceptual framework, postulating both direct and indirect mechanisms that delineate the progression toward technology adoption among educators. The implications extend to the domains of teacher education and professional development.

In the domain of healthcare, Tao et al. (2020) undertook a comprehensive synthesis of prevailing research concerning user acceptance of consumer-oriented health information technologies (CHITs). This endeavour was accomplished through a thorough systematic review and meta-analysis. The research was concentrated on studies that systematically examined the empirical dimensions of user acceptance relevant to CHITs, grounding their analyses within the theoretical frameworks of the Technology Acceptance Model (TAM). The outcomes of this research revealed that TAM indeed serves as a good ground theory for investigating the manifold factors that wield influence over consumer acceptance of CHITs.

Moreover, findings coming from the investigative work of Chauhan and Jaiswal (2017) have substantiated the validity and robustness of the TAM within the domain of research focused on the acceptance of e-health applications. Their study was specifically designed to address a gap in the existing research landscape by offering a comprehensive perspective on the realm of e-health application acceptance research, effectively consolidating insights from relevant literature. Besides, their investigation encompassed a moderator analysis that differentiated between user types and the types of e-health applications. This scrutiny unveiled that the effect size of causal relationships between the variables of TAM is primarily contingent upon the user type, rather than the particular category of e-health application.

Furthermore, the work by Al-Qaysi et al. (2020) encompassed an analysis of studies within the domain of social media, in which the TAM was employed as the primary theoretical model. The primary findings from their research indicated that a predominant research focus pertained to the exploration of social media adoption and utilization patterns among students. Among the studies subject to analysis, a prevailing tendency was the extension of the model through the incorporation of external factors. Noteworthy among these were perceived enjoyment, subjective norm, self-efficacy, perceived critical mass, perceived connectedness, perceived security and perceived trust, which emerged as frequently utilized factors. Additionally, a significant portion of the studies was situated within higher education contexts, with Facebook being established as the most frequently employed social media platform.

In their systematic review, Santini et al. (2019) conducted an analysis of the direct implications of the Technology Acceptance Model (TAM) within the banking sector through the application of meta-analytical structural equation modelling (MASEM). The findings highlighted a strong correlation involving self-efficacy within the TAM framework and underlined a partially mediated connection where attitude intermediates the relationship between TAM and the intention to use technology. The authors posited that investigations which encompass a more comprehensive set of variables within the TAM, conducted within countries with elevated human development indices and a Western orientation, along with heightened Internet penetration and mobile phone usage, exhibit a more pronounced link between ease of use and attitude towards technology. Furthermore, a stronger relationship was observed among users of Internet banking platforms in terms of the interplay between TAM dimensions and their attitudes toward the utilization of electronic banking systems.

A comprehensive review of the literature on the acceptance of video games conducted by Wang and Goh (2017) illuminated the prevailing focal point within game acceptance research, which primarily centres on elucidating the determinants of attitudes and intentions toward engaging in video game play, with a marked under-emphasise on actual usage behaviour. Within their study, video games were catego-rized into two distinct types: hedonic and utilitarian. Their investigation unveiled significant associations between perceived ease of use, perceived usefulness and perceived enjoyment on one hand, and attitude and behavioural intention on the other, among users. Moreover, their findings highlighted the noteworthy influence of respondent type and game platform as significant moderating factors.

Šumak et al. (2017) conducted a quantitative meta-analysis of existing empirical investigations pertaining to the factors influencing the adoption of e-business prac-tices. The primary aim of this study was to analyse the magnitudes of effects associ-ated with factors derived from the Technology Acceptance Model (TAM), while simultaneously identifying the potential moderating influences of consumer type, device type, respondent type and geographical region within these causal relation-ships. The findings substantiated the presence of moderating effects within almost all TAM-associated causal pathways for the four aforementioned factors. Additionally, the study showed that TAM remains the preeminent theoretical frame-work employed within the realm of e-business adoption research.

Due to the escalating adoption of electronic commerce as a credible substitute for conventional shopping practices among a growing consumer base, Ingham et al. (2015) conducted a thorough examination of pertinent literature, delving into the domain of online purchasing acceptance. Within the scope of investigating consum-ers' inclinations toward e-shopping, their study revealed that trust, perceived risk, enjoyment and social influence stand out as the most frequently employed con-structs for the purpose of adapting the Technology Acceptance Model (TAM) to the context of online shopping. Moreover, the study discerned that while the TAM framework significantly contributes to the comprehension of e-shopping behaviour, there exists a potential avenue for enhancing the knowledge base through a more comprehensive exploration of the techno-marketing antecedents that underlie its constituent components.

3.3 Narrative Review of Primary Studies

3.3.1 Conducting the Narrative Review

In order to identify representative primary studies pertaining to the Technology Acceptance Model, a comprehensive systematic narrative review was undertaken in July 2023. The literature review, employing the specified search string (TAM OR "Technology Acceptance Model"), was not bounded by any time-based constraints. In an effort to encompass valuable articles from reputable journals, the search was conducted within the Web of Science Current Contents Connect (CCC) database.

A total of 1.297 peer-reviewed journal articles written in English, wherein "TAM" or "Technology Acceptance Model" appeared within the publication title, were successfully identified. Given the specific focus of this research on the Technology Acceptance Model, the outcomes of the search were refined across four distinct Research Areas of significance:

- Behavioural Sciences
- Computer Science
- Psychology
- Information Science, Library Science

By exclusively considering articles that are applicable to the designated four Research Areas, the aggregate count of journal articles was established at 247, as illustrated in Fig. 3.3.

The titles and abstracts of the identified literature underwent a rigorous screening process to ascertain the pertinence of their content with regard to the specified inclusion criteria. Within this procedure, 25 publications were excluded due to their lack of alignment with the Technology Acceptance Model; these studies involved instances where "TAM" was employed as an abbreviation signifying Therapist Adherence Measure (TAM), Task Abstraction Module (TAM), Test Access Mechanism (TAM), Target Acquisition Module (TAM) and similar terms. To mitigate potential bias, each publication underwent autonomous evaluation by two independent researchers. Instances of disagreement arising during this dual assessment were systematically discussed until a consensus was achieved.

Consequently, unrelated academic literature was excluded, resulting in a refined pool of 222 studies that merited further in-depth analysis. The full texts of these selected works were carefully examined and summarized. Through successive rounds of evaluation, additional publications were eliminated in accordance with

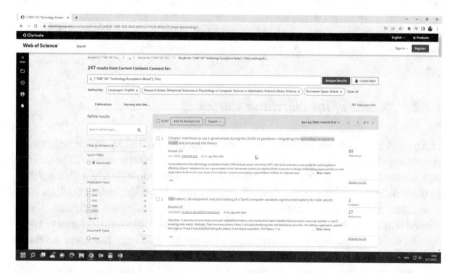

Fig. 3.3 Snapshot depicting the search within the Web of Science Current Contents Connect (WoS CCC) (July 2023)

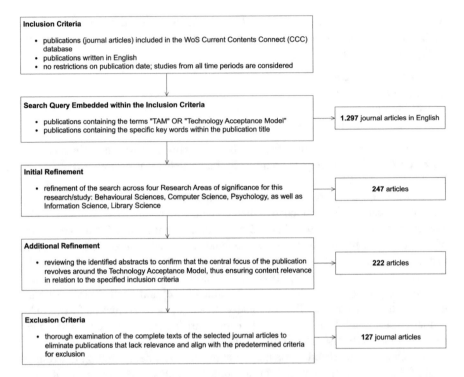

Fig. 3.4 Stages of the selection procedure within the undertaken systematic narrative review of TAM primary studies

the pre-established exclusion criteria, ultimately ending in a total of 127 primary studies that were subjected to thorough assessment and analysis within the scope of this narrative review. The procedural progression of the conducted systematic literature review is elucidated in the flow diagram depicted in Fig. 3.4.

3.3.2 Results of the Narrative Review

The results gathered from the narrative review encompass 127 journal articles, each presenting distinct primary studies supporting this systematic review. These findings are summarized in Table 3.3, and are organized chronologically with emphasis on the most recently conducted research endeavours. The table includes details such as authors' identities, publication years, journals of dissemination and countries of origin for user samples. The "Technology" column provides a comprehensive spectrum of information and communication technology (ICT) products and services. This encompasses a wide array of technological solutions, interactive systems, environments, tools, applications, services and devices employed in the considered studies. In doing so, various contexts and applications associated with the Technology

Table 3.3 Results from the narrative review, encompassing a total of 127 TAM primary studies

Author(s)	Pub-year	Journal	Country	Technology	Sample	Main findings
Papakostas et al.	2023	International Journal of Human–Computer Interaction	Greece	Augmented Reality for Learning	220	Playfulness and quality output as determinants of PU/PEU; quality output predictor of attitude
Zobeidi et al.	2023	Frontiers in Psychology	Iran	E-learning	480	Output quality and Internet anxiety as determinants of PU/PEU; Internet self-efficacy as antecedent of PEU
Tavakoli et al.	2023	The Electronic Library	Iran	Cloud Computing Technology	368	Employee factor and technological factors as determinants of PU/PEU
Ge et al.	2023	Transportation Research Part F	China	Navigation System	372	Trust predictor of attitude and BI; moderating effect of professional driver status on the trust-attitudes relationship
Ren et al.	2022	Frontiers in Psychology	China	Metaverse Technology for Learning	849	Flow experience on BI; moderating effect of gender on the relationship between PEU and BI, attitude and BI, and flow and attitude
Choi	2022	Telematics and Informatics	South Korea	Smart City Technology	239	Compatibility as determinant of PU/PEU; service quality as antecedent of PEU; relative advantage as antecedent of PU
Yu	2022	Frontiers in Psychology	China	Rural Tourism	409	Government trust as determinant of PU/PEU; government trust on BI; moderating effect of perceived risk on the relationship between government trust and PU
Li et al.	2022	Frontiers in Psychology	Taiwan	Augmented Reality with Intangible Cultural Heritage	200	Attitudes and values as determinants of PU; knowledge and understanding, activity, behaviour, and progression, as well as enjoyment, inspiration, and creativity as determinants of PU/PEU

(continued)

Table 3.3 (continued)

Author(s)	Pub-year	Journal	Country	Technology	Sample	Main findings
Chen et al.	2022	International Journal of Industrial Ergonomics	Hong Kong	Virtual Reality Games for Rehabilitation	60	Age as determinant of PU; self-efficacy as determinant of PEU
Wang et al.	2022a	Frontiers in Psychology	China	Short Video Apps for Travel Planning	302	Electronic trust and electronic word of mouth (eWOM) predictors of attitude
Acikgoz and Perez Vega	2022	International Journal of Human–Computer Interaction	USA	Voice Assistant	265	Privacy cynicism predictor of attitude; trust predictor of usage
Acharya and Mekker	2022	Transportation Research PartF	USA	Connected Vehicles	2400	Perceived trust, perceived data privacy and perceived data security as determinants of PU/PEU, as well as predictors of attitude and BI
Sagheer et al.	2022	Frontiers in Psychology	Pakistan	Blockchain Technology (cryptocurrency)	333	Technology awareness as determinants of PU/PEU; perceived risk on BI
Xu et al.	2022	International Journal of Social Robotics	China	AI robots/AI lawyers	385	legal use as determinant of PU/PEU; sense of trust as antecedent of PU and BI
Girish et al.	2022	International Journal of Human–Computer Interaction	India	E-learning	288	e-learning interactivity as determinant of PU/PEU and attitude; uncertainty avoidance and perceived risks of COVID-19 predictors of attitude
Leso and Cortimiglia	2022	Cognition, Technology & Work	Brazil	IS Development	114	Situational involvement and intrinsic involvement as determinant of PU/PEU; intrinsic involvement on BI
Wang et al.	2022b	Frontiers in Psychology	China	Mobile Technology (sports bracelets)	445	Intrinsic sport motivation predictor of attitude
Oyman et al.	2022	Computers in Human Behaviour	Turkey	Augmented Reality in Mobile Applications (cosmetic products)	205	Perceived augmented reality as determinant of PU/PEU; perceived informativeness and perceived enjoyment on BI
Yang et al.	2021	International Journal of Human–Computer Studies	China	Mobile Navigation Applications	384	Sense of direction, navigation application affinity and distraction perception as determinants of PU/PEU, as well as antecedents of BI; navigation application affinity predictor of attitude

Author	Year	Journal	Country	Application	N	Focus
Alexandrakis et al.	2020	International Journal of Human–Computer Interaction	Greece	Web 2.0 Storytelling	112	Future time perspective as determinant of PEU
Baby and Kannammal	2020	Computers in Human Behaviour	India	E-learning	586	Perceived trust on BI
Guner and Acarturk	2020	Universal Access in the Information Society	Turkey	ICT	467	Social influence and anxiety as determinant of PU/PEU
Mir and Padma	2020	Journal of Global Information Technology Management	India	Agricultural Decision Support Systems	265	Social norms on BI
Sagnier et al.	2020	International Journal of Human–Computer Interaction	France	Virtual Reality	89	Pragmatic quality and personal innovativeness as determinants of PU/PEU; cybersickness on BI
Yu and Huang	2020	Electronic Library	China	Smart Libraries	375	Subjective norm on BI
Ahmad et al.	2019	Information Development	Pakistan	E-banking	493	E-service quality as determinant of PU/PEU, attitude, BI and actual usage
Bassiouni et al.	2019	Information Technology & People	UK	Video Games	320	Convenience and ease of use on BI
Lin and Yeh	2019	International Journal of Human–Computer Interaction	China	Virtual Reality for Learning	72	Perceived playfulness as determinant of PU/PEU
Sharma	2019	Information Systems Frontiers	Oman	Mobile Banking	225	Trust and autonomous motivation on BI
Lee et al.	2019	Telematics and Informatics	South Korea	Virtual Reality Devices	350	Perceived enjoyment on BI
Gu et al.	2019	Mobile Information Systems	Pakistan	Mobile-based Tourism Shopping	396	Social presence as determinant of PU/PEU
Verma et al.	2018	Information Processing & Management	India	Big Data Analytics	150	System quality and information quality as determinants of PU/PEU

(continued)

Table 3.3 (continued)

Author(s)	Pub-year	Journal	Country	Technology	Sample	Main findings
Yoon	2018	Computers in Human Behaviour	South Korea	Green IT	267	Descriptive norms and personal norms on BI
Beldad and Hegner	2018	International Journal of Human-Computer Interaction	Germany	Fitness Application	476	Trust and social norm on BI
Chang and Chen	2018	Behaviour & Information Technology	Taiwan	Social Network Games	100	Social norm and customer satisfaction on BI
Guest et al.	2018	Journal of Universal Computer Science	UK	Augmented Reality and Wearable Technologies	142	Performance expectancy, effort expectancy, social influence and hedonic motivation on BI; Facilitating conditions and habit predictors of usage
Razmak and Belanger	2018	Information Technology & People	Canada	Electronic Personal Health Records	325	Communicativeness and compatibility predictive factors of attitude
Makki et al.	2018	International Journal of Human-Computer Interaction	USA	Social Network	236	Perceived playfulness, subjective norm and critical mass predictors of usage
Kanak and Sogukpinar	2017	IET Biometrics	Turkey	Biometric Authentication Systems	50	Trust as determinant of PU/PEU
Sanchez-Prieto et al.	2017	Computers in Human Behaviour	Spain	M-learning	678	Self-efficacy as determinant of PU/PEU
Wu and Chen	2017	Computers in Human Behaviour	China	Massive Open Online Courses	252	Openness, reputation, social motivation and social influence as determinants of PU/PEU
Zainab et al.	2017	Behaviour & Information Technology	Saudi Arabia	E-training	450	Perceived cost predictor of usage
Rigopoulou et al.	2017	International Journal of Mobile Communications	Greece	Smartphone	310	Social and materialistic values on BI
Xie et al.	2017	Electronic Library	China	E-government	268	Risk and trust predictors of attitude; Perceived behaviour control and subjective norm on BI

Chen et al.	2017	Mobile Information Systems	China	Mobile Social Gaming Service	491	Perceived enjoyment predictor of attitude; flow on BI
Yoon	2016	Journal of Academic Librarianship	South Korea	Mobile Library Applications	273	Perceived interactivity predictive factor of attitude; satisfaction on BI
Lin and Kim	2016	Computers in Human Behaviour	USA	Social Media	536	Intrusiveness concerns and privacy concerns predictors of attitude; privacy concerns on BI
Ooi and Tan	2016	Expert Systems with Applications	Malaysia	Smartphone Credit Card	459	Trust and compatibility on BI
Abdullah et al.	2016	Computers in Human Behaviour	UK	E-portfolios	242	Experience, subjective norm, enjoyment and self-efficacy as determinants of PU/PEU
Chang et al.	2016	International Journal of Mobile Communications	South Korea	Wearable Device	342	Perceived privacy, subjective norm and wearability on BI
Park and Kwon	2016	Program-Electronic Library and Information Systems	South Korea	Teaching Assistant Robots	609	Perceived enjoyment and service quality as determinants of PU/PEU
Kwee-Meier et al.	2016	Behaviour & Information Technology	Germany	Wearable Locating Systems	2086	Social influence, privacy concern and perceived security risk on BI
Chen et al.	2016	Electronic Library	Taiwan	Digital Library	264	User satisfaction predictor of attitude
Dogruel et al.	2015	Behaviour & Information Technology	Germany	New Media Entertainment Technology	240	Enjoyment predictive factor of attitude
Cheng et al.	2015	Computer Standards & Interfaces	Taiwan	E-portfolio System	360	Gender, grade level and willingness to share as moderators
Akman and Mishra	2015	Computers in Human Behaviour	Turkey	Green IT	182	Subjective norms and level of awareness as determinants of PU/PEU
Park et al.	2015	Behaviour & Information Technology	South Korea	Car Navigation System	1045	Service and display quality predictors of attitude and BI
Hsiao et al.	2015	LIBRI	Taiwan	E-textbooks	312	Perceived enjoyment predictive factor of attitude

(continued)

Table 3.3 (continued)

Author(s)	Pub-year	Journal	Country	Technology	Sample	Main findings
Mohammadi	2015	Computers in Human Behaviour	Iran	E-learning	390	Satisfaction predictor of usage; educational quality, service quality, technical system quality, content and information quality on BI
Jin	2014	Computers in Human Behaviour	South Korea	E-book	1030	Compatibility, relative advantage, self-efficacy, and subjective norms as determinants of PU/PEU
Jongchul and Sung-Joon	2014	Telematics and Informatics	South Korea	Haptic Enabling Technology (HET)	254	Relative advantage, compatibility and presence as determinants of PU/PEU
Park et al.	2014	Computers in Human Behaviour	South Korea	Teleconferencing System	155	Anxiety predictor of usage
Calisir et al.	2014	Human Factors and Ergonomics in Manufacturing & Service Industries	Turkey	Web-based Learning System	546	Perceived content quality, perceived system quality and anxiety as determinants of PU/PEU
Cegarra et al.	2014	International Journal of Information Management	Spain	E-government	307	Attitude as predictor of usage
Park and Kim	2014	Telematics and Informatics	South Korea	Mobile Cloud Computing Services	1099	Satisfaction on BI; perceived connectedness and perceived security predictor of attitude
Chen and Chan	2014	Ergonomics	Hong Kong	Gerontechnology Products	1012	Facilitating conditions predictor of attitude; Gerontechnology self-efficacy, gerontechnology anxiety, health conditions, cognitive ability, social relationships, attitude to life and satisfaction, physical functioning predictors of usage
Park and Kim	2014	Personal and Ubiquitous Computing	South Korea	Car Navigation System	1181	perceived connectedness and perceived security predictors of attitude; satisfaction on BI
Park et al.	2014	Telematics and Informatics	South Korea	Mobile Social Network Games	20	Perceived enjoyment and perceived connectedness predictors of attitude; Perceived mobility and satisfaction on BI

Joo and Sang	2013	Computers in Human Behaviour	South Korea	Smartphone	491	Motivation as moderator between PU/PEU and BI
Choi and Chung	2013	International Journal of Human-Computer Interaction	USA	Social Networking Sites	179	Subjective norm on BI
Svendsen et al.	2013	Behaviour & Information Technology	Norway	Software Tool	1004	Personality traits on BI
Kashi and Zheng	2013	International Journal of Selection and Assessment	Iran	E-recruitment	332	Impressions of website and impressions of hiring organization on BI
Lee et al.	2013	Behaviour & Information Technology	Taiwan	E-learning	365	Organisational support, computer self-efficacy, prior experience and task equivocality as determinants of PU/PEU
Park and Kim	2013	Program-Electronic Library and Information Systems	South Korea	Long-Term Evolution Services	1344	Perceived adaptivity, and system & service quality predictors of attitude; satisfaction on BI
Kim	2012	Electronic Library	South Korea	Social Software	116	Communication and knowledge sharing determinants of PU
Shyu and Huang	2011	Government Information Quarterly	Taiwan	E-government	307	Perceived enjoyment predictive factor of attitude
Sipior et al.	2011	European Journal of Information Systems	USA	E-government	37	Access barriers predictor of usage
Chen and Chen	2011	Expert Systems with Applications	Taiwan	GPS Technology	251	Perceived enjoyment predictor of attitude; Personal innovativeness moderates the relationship between attitude and BI
Jan and Contreras	2011	Computers in Human Behaviour	Peru	IT in Universities	89	Subjective norm predictive factor of attitude
Sheikhshoaei and Oloumi	2011	Electronic Library	Iran	IT in Libraries	160	All independent variables in the TAM framework (PU, PEU and attitude) affect acceptance

(continued)

Table 3.3 (continued)

Author(s)	Pub-year	Journal	Country	Technology	Sample	Main findings
Alshare et al.	2011	Journal of Global Information Technology Management	USA	Computers	491	National culture as moderator of TAM variables
Lee and Chang	2011	Journal of Computer-Mediated Communication	South Korea	Online Co-design Process	749	Perceived enjoyment and perceived control predictor of attitude
Egea and González	2022	Computers in Human Behaviour	Spain	Electronic Health Care Records	254	Trust predictive factor of attitude
Lee and Wan	2010	Data Base for Advances in Information Systems	China	E-ticketing	194	Trust on BI
Sanchez and Hueros	2010	Computers in Human Behaviour	Spain	Moodle	226	Computer self-efficacy predictor of attitude
Nayak et al.	2010	Universal Access in the Information Society	UK	Internet	592	Good health predictor of usage (moderated by age)
Pan and Jordan-Marsh	2010	Computers in Human Behaviour	USA	Internet	374	Subjective norm predictor of usage; subjective norm and facilitating conditions on BI; age as moderator
Yousafzai et al.	2010	Journal of Applied Social Psychology	UK	Internet Banking	441	Trust on BI; perceived security and perceived privacy predictors of usage
Djamasbi et al.	2010	Decision Support Systems	USA	Decision Support Systems	134	Positive mood on BI
Tzou and Lu	2009	Behaviour & Information Technology	Taiwan	Fashion Technology	304	Beauty and pleasure on BI; uniqueness as moderator
Chiu et al.	2009	Behaviour & Information Technology	Taiwan	Online Shopping	311	PU and satisfaction on BI
Shin	2009	Behaviour & Information Technology	USA	IPTV	571	System quality and content quality predictors of attitude; social pressure on BI

Author	Year	Journal	Country	Technology	n	Findings
Kim and Garrison	2009	Information Systems Frontiers	South Korea	Mobile Wireless Technology	862	Perceived ubiquity, perceived reachability and job relevance determinants of BI
Park et al.	Park et al., 2009	International Journal of Information Management	USA	Digital Library	1082	PEU significantly impacts PU, leading to BI
Lee	2009	Electronic Commerce Research and Applications	Taiwan	Online Banking	368	Perceived risk and perceived benefit predictors of attitude and BI
Lu et al.	2009	Computers in Human Behaviour	China	Instant Messaging	250	Perceived enjoyment predictor of attitude; Perceived behavioural control, concentration and subjective norm on BI
Shin	2009	International Journal of Human-Computer Interaction	South Korea	Digital Multimedia Broadcasting	269	Perceived availability and the perceived cost level on BI
Tung et al.	2009	Social Behaviour and Personality	Taiwan	Customer Relationship Management IS	288	Compatibility, trust and perceived financial cost on BI
Bueno and Salmeron	2008	Interacting with Computers	Spain	ERP Systems	91	Cooperation as determinant of PU; training and technological complexity as determinants of PEU
Lopez-Nicolas et al.	2008	Information & Management	Netherlands	3G-Related Technologies	542	Social influence and perceived benefits on BI
Kim and Forsythe	2008	Psychology & Marketing	USA	Sensory Enabling Technologies	354	Technology anxiety predictor of usage
Stern et al.	2008	Psychology & Marketing	USA	Online auctions	329	Affinity with the computer as determinant of PU/PEU; risk tolerance and impulsiveness on BI
Shin and Kim	2008	Cyberpsychology & Behaviour	South Korea	Web 2.0	352	Perceived synchronicity predictor of attitude; perceived enjoyment on BI
Yoon and Kim	2007	Electronic Commerce Research and Applications	South Korea	Wireless LAN	161	Perceived convenience as determinant of PU

(continued)

Table 3.3 (continued)

Author(s)	Pub-year	Journal	Country	Technology	Sample	Main findings
Huang et al.	2007	Electronic Library	Taiwan	Mobile Learning	313	Perceived enjoyment and perceived mobility on BI
Cheung and Sachs	2006	Psychological Reports	Hong Kong	Web-Based IS	57	Self-efficacy predictor of usage; enjoyment as determinant of PU/PEU
Burton-Jones and Hubona	2006	Information & Management	USA	Email, Word	125	Age, level of education and system experience as determinants of PU/PEU
McFarland and Hamilton	2006	Computers in Human Behaviour	USA	IT	114	Computer anxiety, prior experience, other's use, organizational support, task structure, system quality, and PU predictors of usage
Yu et al.	2005	Information & Management	South Korea	T-commerce	1001	Perceived enjoyment predictor of attitude and BI
Wu and Wang	2005	Information & Management	Taiwan	Mobile Commerce	850	Perceived risk, cost, compatibility on BI
Wu and Chen	2005	International Journal of Human-Computer Studies	Taiwan	Online Tax	1032	Trust and subjective norm on BI
Saade and Bahli	2005	Information & Management	Canada	Online Learning	102	Cognitive absorption on BI
Lai and Li	2005	Information & Management	Hong Kong	Internet Banking	32	Gender, age and IT competency on BI
Yang and Yoo	2004	Decision Support Systems	South Korea	IS	211	Cognitive attitude predictor of usage
Hsu and Lu	2004	Information & Management	Taiwan	Online Games	233	Social norms, attitudes, and flow experience on BI
Shih	2004	Information & Management	Taiwan	Internet	203	The relevance of information as determinants of PU/PEU and attitude
Amoako-Gyampah and Salam	2004	Information & Management	USA	ERP Technology	40	Shared beliefs as determinant of PU/PEU

Author	Year	Journal	Country	Application		Findings
Vijayasarathy	2004	Information & Management	USA	Online Shopping	281	Compatibility, usefulness, ease of use, and security predictive factors of attitude
Pikkarainen et al.	2004	Internet Research	Finland	Online Banking	268	PU and information on online banking predictors of usage
Spacey et al.	2004	Journal of Documentation	UK	Internet	26	Subjective norm as determinant of PU, attitude and intention
Yi and Hwang	2004	International Journal of Human-Computer Studies	USA	Web-Based IS	109	Enjoyment as determinant of PU/PEU; self-efficacy predictor of usage
Horton et al.	2001	Journal of Information Technology	UK	Intranet	386	Self-report and actual measures of usage are not interchangeable when applying the TAM model
Moon and Kim	2001	Information & Management	South Korea	WWW	152	Perceived playfulness on BI
Lederer et al.	2000	Decision Support Systems	USA	WWW	163	Ease of understanding and ease of finding as determinants of PEU; Information quality as determinant of PU
Roberts and Henderson	2000	Interacting with Computers	Australia	IT in the Workplace	108	PU and perceived fun predictors of usage
Hu et al.	1999	Journal of Management Information Systems	Hong Kong	Telemedicine	421	Perceived playfulness on BI
Gefen and Straub	1997	MIS Quarterly	Japan	Email	392	Gender as determinant of PU/PEU

Legend:
BI   Behavioural Intention
PU   Perceived Usefulness
PEU   Perceived Ease of Use
ICT   Information and Communication Technology
IS   Information System
IT   Information Technology
ERP   Enterprise Resource Planning

Acceptance Model (TAM) and its extensions, referred to as "TAM++", become apparent. This association reflects the overarching trajectory of technological advancement and scientific inquiries into the acceptance and adoption of specific technologies. The table concludes with information on user sample sizes and principal findings from each study, providing a comprehensive compilation of data.

The main findings derived from the evaluated and analysed studies, as identified within this systematic review, have been categorized into four distinct groupings:

- Determinants of usefulness and ease of use
- Predictive factors of attitude
- Antecedents of behavioural intention
- Predictors of usage

The categorizations are established based on the research models and frameworks presented in the chosen journal articles, supplemented by the posited hypotheses and empirically validated outcomes. These categorizations are subsequently presented below.

(a) *Determinants of Usefulness and Ease of Use*

Self-efficacy, a considerably examined variable within the domain of technology acceptance, has gathered support from Jin (2014), Abdullah et al. (2016) and Sanchez-Prieto et al. (2017) as a reliable predictor of both perceived ease of use and perceived usefulness. Additionally, the recognition of self-efficacy as an antecedent of perceived ease of use has been apparent in the investigation of virtual reality games for rehabilitation (Chen et al., 2022) and within the context of e-learning systems (Zobeidi et al., 2023).

The construct of *enjoyment*, acknowledged as a well-established variable, was explored by Yi and Hwang (2004), along with Cheung and Sachs (2006), who identified it as a determinant influencing both the perceived usefulness and ease of use of web-based information systems. Consistent outcomes were obtained in the investigation pertaining to teaching assistant robots, as demonstrated in the study conducted by Park and Kwon (2016). Furthermore, *perceived playfulness* was observed to exert an impact on the perceived usefulness and ease of use of educational virtual reality (Lin & Yeh, 2019) and augmented reality for learning, as revealed by the recent study of Papakostas et al. (2023).

Investigations into technology domains characterized by significant privacy concerns, such as digital or virtual lawyers (Xu et al., 2022), biometric authentication systems (Kanak & Sogukpinar, 2017) and online tax systems (Wu & Chen, 2005), have highlighted the paramount role of *trust* as a vital antecedent to the perceptions of usefulness and ease of use. Moreover, the study focusing on public acceptance of connected vehicles conducted by Acharya and Mekker (2022) identified *perceived trust*, along with *perceived data privacy and security*, as antecedents of perceived usefulness and perceived ease of use.

In their research, Chen et al. (2022) concentrated on virtual reality games for rehabilitation and identified *age* as an antecedent of perceived usefulness. On the other hand, Burton-Jones and Hubona (2006) introduced several individual variables, including *age, educational attainment* and *experience with email*, high-lighting their significant impact on ease of use and perceived usefulness. The sig-nificance of *prior experience* as a determinant factor has been underscored in the investigations conducted by Lee et al. (2013) and Abdullah et al. (2016), respec-tively, in the contexts of e-learning systems and e-portfolios acceptance.

Furthermore, diverse aspects of various technology systems were subject to examination, such as web-based learning systems (Calisir et al., 2014), big data analytics (Verma et al., 2018) and augmented reality for learning (Papakostas et al., 2023) with *content, system* and *output quality* emerging as important antecedents to perceived usefulness and perceived ease of use. Furthermore, within the realm of e-learning systems, a recent study conducted by Zobeidi et al. (2023) has brought to light the emergence of *output quality* and *Internet anxiety* as antecedents of per-ceived usefulness and perceived ease of use, alongside the identification of *Internet self-efficacy* as a predictor of perceived ease of use. Lee et al. (2013) further deter-mined that *organizational support, computer self-efficacy* and the *task equivocality* exerted a positive influence on ease of use and perceived usefulness within their study.

In the context of embracing the World Wide Web, Lederer et al. (2000) posited the constructs of *ease of understanding* and *ease of finding* as predictive variables for ease of use, with *information quality* emerging as a predictor of perceived use-fulness. Moreover, Shih (2004) underscored the *relevance of information* as a strong determinant influencing the perceived usefulness and ease of use within the context of Internet acceptance.

Besides, Akman and Mishra (2015) pointed to the role of the *level of awareness* as a predictive factor concerning the two core constructs of the TAM model in the context of adopting green information technology. Additionally, Sagheer et al. (2022) identified *technology awareness* as an antecedent of perceived usefulness and perceived ease of use while investigating the adoption and usage of cryptocur-rency. Focusing on the domain of Haptic Enabling Technology (HET), Jongchul and Sung-Joon (2014) unveiled variables such as *relative advantage, compatibility* and *presence* as antecedences to the perceived usefulness and ease of use. In a simi-lar manner, Bueno and Salmeron (2008) explored the context of ERP technology, revealing *cooperation* as a determinant of perceived usefulness, alongside *training* and *technological complexity* as factors impacting the perceived ease of use.

During their research into the adoption of mobile navigation applications, Yang et al. (2021) identified antecedents of perceived usefulness and perceived ease of use as *sense of direction, navigation application affinity* and perception of distrac-tion (*distraction perception*). Furthermore, in the specific context of addressing aug-mented reality within mobile applications, Oyman et al. (2022) identified *perceived augmented reality* as an antecedent of perceived usefulness and perceived ease of use. The research by Sagnier et al. (2020) explained that *pragmatic quality and personal innovativeness* influence the perceived usefulness and perceived ease of use attributed to virtual reality devices.

Influence comes from training and project communication in shaping the collective beliefs of users regarding the advantages associated with enterprise resource planning (ERP) technology. These *shared beliefs*, in turn, exert an influence on the perceived usefulness and ease of use of the technology itself, as elucidated by Amoako-Gyampah and Salam (2004).

One of the variables subjected to comprehensive examination pertains to the *subjective norm*. Its correlation with usefulness within the context of adopting Internet usage has been investigated (Spacey et al., 2004). Moreover, this particular construct has demonstrated its predictive capabilities concerning the core constructs of the TAM model in diverse studies, including e-book adoption (Jin, 2014), e-portfolio acceptance (Abdullah et al., 2016) and the adoption of green information technology as emphasized by Akman and Mishra (2015).

Openness, reputation, social motivation and *social influence* have been identified as antecedent factors in the investigation by Wu and Chen (2017), introducing new social variables within the context of exploring Massive Open Online Courses (MOOCs) as a specific form of educational technology. Furthermore, the work of Guner and Acarturk (2020) established that factors such as *social influence* and *anxiety* play a predictive role in shaping perceptions toward information and communication technologies at large.

(b) *Predictive Factors of Attitude*

When investigating the disposition towards technology platforms that facilitate social interactions, researchers frequently incorporate variables such as *user satisfaction* (Chen et al., 2016) and *enjoyment* into their models. This practice is particularly evident in studies pertaining to electronically mediated commerce using interactive television (i.e. t-commerce) (Yu et al., 2005), instant messaging (Lu et al., 2009), online co-design processes (Lee & Chang, 2011), Global Positioning System (GPS) technology (Chen & Chen, 2011), mobile social network games (Park et al., 2014), e-Textbooks (Hsiao et al., 2015), new media entertainment technology (Dogruel et al., 2015) and mobile social gaming services (Chen et al., 2017).

Specific demographic variables and competencies have also emerged as predictive factors within specific contexts. For instance, in the investigation by Lai and Li (2005), *gender, age* and proficiency in information technology (*information technology competency*) emerged as significant determinants shaping individuals' attitudes toward adopting Internet banking. Wang et al. (2022a, b), in their study focused on mobile technology — specifically sports bracelets — identified *intrinsic sport motivation* as a notable predictor of attitudes. Moreover, the work by Sanchez and Hueros (2010) has emphasised the role of *computer self-efficacy* as a determinant shaping attitudes towards e-learning platforms.

The attitude towards utilizing technology, particularly in contexts characterized by privacy or security implications, has been substantiated to be influenced by several factors. *Intrusiveness concerns* and *privacy concerns*, notably within the realm of social media utilization, contribute to shaping particular attitude (Lin & Kim, 2016). *Privacy cynicism* has been identified as predictor of attitude in a study dealing with the acceptance of voice assistants (Acikgoz & Perez Vega, 2022).

In the context of addressing challenges posed by the COVID-19 pandemic within educational environments, the investigation conducted by Girish et al. (2022) explained that predictors such as *uncertainty avoidance* and *perceived risks of COVID-19* influence individuals' attitudes toward e-learning systems. *Perceived security*, in relation to online shopping, has been demonstrated to impact this attitude (Vijayasarathy, 2004), as well as in the context of car navigation systems (Park & Kim, 2014). Similarly, *perceived risk* pertaining to online banking has also been identified as a determinant (Lee, 2009).

Moreover, the level of *trust*, a comprehensively studied variable, has been found to play a significant role in shaping attitudes towards a range of technologies, including navigation systems (Ge et al., 2023), short video apps for travel planning (Wang et al. 2022a, b), electronic health care records (Egea & González, 2022), connected vehicles (Acharya & Mekker, 2022) and e-government services (Xie et al., 2017). Additionally, the *subjective norm* has been identified as a determinant of the attitude towards using the Internet (Spacey et al., 2004) as well as information technology (Jan & Contreras, 2011).

Researchers frequently conduct investigations into distinct technological domains, and in doing so, they incorporate specific variables into their research models that possess predictive potency concerning attitudes. For instance, the *perceived synchronicity* of web 2.0 has been considered within this context (Shin & Kim, 2008), as has the *perceived adaptivity* of long-term evolution services (Park & Kim, 2013). The concept of *perceived connectedness* has been explored in relation to teleconferencing systems (Park et al., 2014), and the *perceived interactivity* of a mobile library application has been incorporated into similar studies (Yoon, 2016).

Moreover, dimensions associated with system quality play a substantial role. The *content* quality of digital multimedia interfaces, for instance, has been underscored as a determinant of attitude (Shin, 2009), while *display* quality has been associated with the attitude towards car navigation systems (Park et al., 2015). Additionally, the affinity for navigation applications (*navigation application affinity*) was highlighted as a determinant influencing individuals' attitudes toward mobile navigation applications in the study conducted by Yang et al. (2021).

(c) *Antecedents of Behavioural Intention*

The quest to identify antecedents to behavioural intention is inherently guided by the particular context of technology acceptance. Within this context, *perceived playfulness* emerges as an antecedent influencing behavioural intention towards using the World Wide Web (Moon & Kim, 2001). Similarly, the determinant of *perceived enjoyment* holds influence over behavioural intention in relation to diverse technological domains, such as augmented reality in mobile applications (in particular, cosmetic products) (Oyman et al., 2022), t-commerce (Yu et al., 2005), m-learning (Huang et al., 2007), virtual reality devices (Lee et al., 2019) and web 2.0 (Shin & Kim, 2008).

Furthermore, the variable of *user satisfaction* assumes significance across various studies as a predictor of behavioural intention. Noteworthy instances include its predictive role for the intention to utilize mobile social network games

(Park et al., 2014), car navigation system (Park & Kim, 2014), mobile library applications (Yoon, 2016), and long-term evolution (LTE) services (Park & Kim, 2013). Additionally, the factor of *convenience* is identified as a determinant influencing the intention to engage with video games (Bassiouni et al., 2019).

Significant attention has been directed towards specific individual characteristics in the exploration of factors affecting behavioural intention. Certain elements have emerged as focal points, including the role of *positive mood* within the context of decision support systems (Djamasbi et al., 2010). Moreover, *personality traits* have been recognized as influential factors, exerting an impact on the acceptance of software tools (Svendsen et al., 2013).

Explorations into the domain of technology acceptance have also highlighted the significance of psychological factors. Notably, concepts such as *flow experience* within metaverse technology for learning (Ren et al., 2022) and *cognitive absorption* within online learning have drawn attention (Saade & Bahli, 2005), showcasing their potential to shape behavioural intention. Meanwhile, studies conducted within the context of information system development have underscored the significance of *intrinsic involvement* in influencing behavioural intention (Leso & Cortimiglia, 2022).

Moreover, the work by Lai and Li (2005) has found the relevance of *gender*, *age* and *information technology (IT) competency* as determinants shaping behavioural intention concerning Internet banking. Additionally, the intention to engage in online shopping has demonstrated a strong association with factors such as *attitude* toward online shopping, *normative beliefs* and *self-efficacy* (Vijayasarathy, 2004).

Behavioural intention within various technological contexts has been illuminated by an array of determinants. In the domain of mobile commerce, for instance, factors encompassing *perceived risk*, *cost* and *compatibility* have been identified as determinants of behavioural intention (Wu & Wang, 2005). Similarly, the intention to engage in online auctions has been found to be shaped by *risk tolerance* and *impulsiveness* (Stern et al., 2008).

Meanwhile, research endeavours focused on online banking have highlighted the influential role of *perceived risk* and *perceived benefit* in shaping intention (Lee, 2009). Within the framework of wearable locating systems, behavioural intention has been linked to factors including *perceived security risk*, *social influence* and *privacy concerns* (Kwee-Meier et al., 2016). The impact of *perceived risk* on intention was identified in a study conducted within the domain of blockchain technology, specifically concerning the use of cryptocurrency (Sagheer et al., 2022).

Studies into e-learning platforms, as conducted by Baby and Kannammal (2020), have explored the significance of *perceived trust*. Furthermore, the concept of trust has emerged as a well-observed variable examined within the context of technologies that involve sensitive matters, including but not limited to Internet banking (Yousafzai et al., 2010), mobile banking (Sharma, 2019), e-ticketing (Lee & Wan, 2010) and smartphone credit card usage (Ooi & Tan, 2016). Furthermore, the role of *trust* has been recognized as a determinant shaping the behavioural intention of drivers in the adoption of navigation systems (Ge et al., 2023) and connected vehicles (Acharya & Mekker, 2022). Moreover, the *sense of trust* has been found to influence the usage of AI robots in the context of AI lawyers (Xu et al., 2022) and to impact government trust among farm households engaged in rural tourism (Yu, 2022). Besides, the domain of customer relationship management information systems has unveiled the significance of factors such as *compatibility*, *trust* and *perceived financial cost* in driving behavioural intention (Tung et al., 2009).

Additionally, the *perceived availability* and *perceived cost level* of digital multimedia broadcasting have been shown to influence behavioural intention (Shin, 2009). Likewise, the *perceived ubiquity* and *perceived reachability* of mobile wireless technology have demonstrated a similar influence (Kim & Garrison, 2009). In the context of augmented reality and wearable technologies, factors such as *performance expectancy*, *effort expectancy*, *social influence* and *hedonic motivation* have been found to be relevant determinants (Guest et al., 2018). Besides, Mohammadi (2015) has proposed antecedents including *educational quality*, *service quality* and *technical system quality*, along with *content and information quality* in relation to behavioural intention.

Within the framework of technologies with implications for human communication and interaction, there are two diffusion-related variables, namely *social influence* and *perceived benefits* associated with advanced mobile services, particularly in terms of flexibility and status. These variables have been recognized as antecedents to behavioural intention, as explicated in the study by Lopez-Nicolas et al. (2008).

Furthermore, the constructs of *subjective norm* and *social norm* emerge as robust determinants influencing behavioural intention. This is evident in studies exploring instant messaging (Lu et al., 2009), social networking sites (Choi & Chung, 2013), social network games (Chang & Chen, 2018), smart libraries (Yu & Huang, 2020) and fitness applications (Beldad & Hegner, 2018). The study conducted by Hsu and Lu (2004) demonstrated that *social norms*, *attitudes* and the *flow experience* collectively accounted for approximately 80% of the observed variance in intent to play online games.

(d) *Predictors of Usage*

Researchers have also investigated the actual use of technologies and its associated predictors. The relationship between the constructs within the TAM framework demonstrated its utmost strength when modelled using conventionally collected self-reported usage data. Nevertheless, a somewhat weakened relationship among the variables persisted even when modelled with actual usage data, as illustrated by the findings in studies such as that of Horton et al. (2001).

The theoretical framework of computer acceptance posits that *perceived usefulness* and *perceived enjoyment* have the potential to yield positive effects on both facets of acceptance — satisfaction and usage, as proposed by Roberts and Henderson (2000). Furthermore, the empirical investigation conducted by Mohammadi in 2015 exposed a significant impact of *satisfaction* on the usage of e-learning technology. Additionally, within the realm of consumer behaviour analysis, Acikgoz and Perez Vega' study in 2022 specified the role of *trust* as a predictor of voice assistant usage.

Self-efficacy emerged as a strong determinant of usage within web-based information systems, as observed in studies by Yi and Hwang (2004) and Cheung and Sachs (2006). In their investigation, McFarland and Hamilton (2006) revealed that system utilization is significantly influenced by factors such as *computer anxiety*, *prior experience*, the observed usage of others (*other's use*), *organizational support*, the structure of tasks (*task structure*), the quality of the system (*system quality*) as well as *perceived usefulness*.

In a study conducted by Pikkarainen et al. (2004), the main factors driving the acceptance of online banking were identified as *perceived usefulness* and access to relevant information (*information on online banking*). Additionally, the embracement and utilization of Internet banking were found to be predicted by *perceived security* and *perceived privacy*, as underscored in the research by Yousafzai et al. (2010). Lastly, Ahmad et al. (2019) ascertained that the quality of e-services (*e-service quality*) played a significant role in predicting the usage of electronic banking services.

3.4   The TAM Universe

Upon careful examination of the final selection, comprising 127 primary studies forming the foundation of research centred on the core model and its extensions ("TAM++"), several noteworthy observations have come to light. The first aspect involves the global prevalence of authors showing considerable interest in exploring the Technology Acceptance Model. These authors have conducted investigations on the core model and its various versions across a multitude of contexts, encompassing diverse user types, sample sizes, and a comprehensive spectrum of information and communication technology (ICT) products and services. As depicted in Fig. 3.5, this scholarly endeavour involves distinct cultural settings united by a shared objective — to examine users' adoption patterns of diverse technologies. Furthermore, it aims to interpret user behaviour during engagements with a range of technologies and services that facilitate communication and the exchange of information in various forms.

A significant proportion of research contributions originates from Asian regions. Countries such as South Korea, Taiwan, China and Hong Kong have conducted extensive assessments to unveil the potential of numerous technologies in various contextual scenarios and applications. Simultaneously, North America and Europe also pursue similar objectives, approaching research with comparable perspectives.

The subsequent consideration pertains to the varying sample sizes of participant users featured within the selected primary studies, as demonstrated by the sample size distribution showcased in Fig. 3.6. In a substantial majority of the examined research (specifically amounting to 80.3%), the sampled population

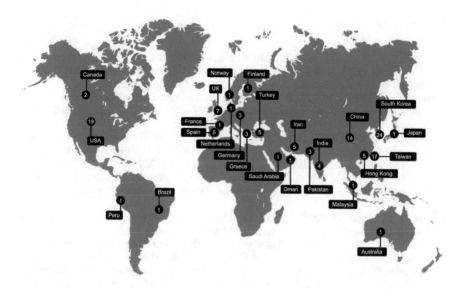

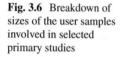

Fig. 3.5 Global prevalence of TAM research and corresponding number of selected studies

Fig. 3.6 Breakdown of sizes of the user samples involved in selected primary studies

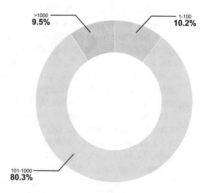

encompassed a range of 101 to 1000 users, while 10.2% of the aggregate sample groups constituted fewer than 101 participants. Additionally, only 9.5% of all studies encompassed participant counts surpassing 1000 users. This empirical distribution attests to the extensive and comprehensive efforts invested by researchers in the domain of technology acceptance and the investigation of the TAM model. Furthermore, the results, supported by statistical methodologies aligned with these diverse sample sizes, reveal a robust foundation for the conclusions drawn by these researchers.

References

Abdullah, F., Ward, R., & Ahmed, E. (2016). Investigating the influence of the most commonly used external variables of TAM on students' Perceived Ease of Use (PEOU) and Perceived Usefulness (PU) of e-portfolios. *Computers in Human Behavior, 63*, 75–90.

Acharya, S., & Mekker, M. (2022). Public acceptance of connected vehicles: An extension of the technology acceptance model. *Transportation Research Part F: Traffic Psychology and Behaviour, 88*, 54–68. https://doi.org/10.1016/j.trf.2022.05.002

Acikgoz, F., & Perez Vega, R. (2022). The role of privacy cynicism in consumer habits with voice assistants: A technology acceptance model perspective. *International Journal of Human–Computer Interaction, 38*(12), 1138–1152. https://doi.org/10.1080/10447318.2021.1987677

Ahmad, S., Bhatti, S. H., & Hwang, Y. (2019). E-service quality and actual use of e-banking: Explanation through the technology acceptance model. *Information Development, 36*(4), 503–519.

Akman, I., & Mishra, A. (2015). Sector diversity in green information technology practices: Technology acceptance model perspective. *Computers in Human Behavior, 49*, 477–486.

Al-Emran, M., Mezhuyev, V., & Kamaludin, A. (2018). Technology acceptance model in m-learning context: A systematic review. *Computers & Education, 125*, 1–41.

Alexandrakis, D., Chorianopoulos, K., & Tselios, N. (2020). Older adults and web 2.0 storytelling technologies: Probing the technology acceptance model through an age-related perspective. *International Journal of Human-Computer Interaction, 36*(17), 1–13.

Al-Qaysi, N., Mohamad-Nordin, N., & Al-Emran, M. (2020). Employing the technology acceptance model in social media: A systematic review. *Education and Information Technologies.* https://doi.org/10.1007/s10639-020-10197-1

Al-Qaysi, N., Granić, A., Al-Emran, M., Ramayah, T., Garces, E., & Daim, T. U. (2023). Social media adoption in education: A systematic review of disciplines, applications, and influential factors. *Technology in society, 73*, 102249. https://doi.org/10.1016/j.techsoc.2023.102249

Alshare, K. A., Mesak, H. I., Grandon, E. E., & Badri, M. A. (2011). Examining the moderating role of national culture on an extended technology acceptance model. *Journal of Global Information Technology Management, 14*(3), 27–53.

Amoako-Gyampah, K., & Salam, A. F. (2004). An extension of the technology acceptance model in an ERP implementation environment. *Information & Management, 41*(6), 731–745.

Baby, A., & Kannammal, A. (2020). Network path analysis for developing an enhanced TAM model: A user- centric e-learning perspective. *Computers in Human Behavior, 107*, 1–7.

Bassiouni, D. H., Hackley, C., & Meshreki, H. (2019). The integration of video games in family-life dynamics: An adapted technology acceptance model of family intention to consume video games. *Information Technology & People, 32*(6), 1376–1396.

Beldad, A. D., & Hegner, S. M. (2018). Expanding the technology acceptance model with the inclusion of trust, social influence, and health valuation to determine the predictors of german users' willingness to continue using a fitness app: A structural equation modelling approach. *International Journal of Human-Computer Interaction, 34*(9), 882–893.

Bueno, S., & Salmeron, J. L. (2008). TAM-based success modelling in ERP. *Interacting with Computers, 20*(6), 515–523.

Burton-Jones, A., & Hubona, G. S. (2006). The mediation of external variables in the technology acceptance model. *Information & Management, 43*, 706–717.

Calisir, F., Gumussoy, C. A., Bayraktaroglu, A. E., & Karaali, D. (2014). Predicting the intention to use a web-based learning system: Perceived content quality, anxiety, perceived system quality, image, and the technology acceptance model. *Human Factors and Ergonomics in Manufacturing & Service Industries, 24*(5), 515–531.

Cegarra, J. L. M., Navarro, J. G. C., & Pachón, J. R. C. (2014). Applying the technology acceptance model to a Spanish City Hall. *International Journal of Information Management, 34*(4), 437–445.

Chang, C.-C., & Chen, P.-Y. (2018). Analysis of critical factors for social games based on extended technology acceptance model: A DEMATEL approach. *Behaviour & Information Technology, 37*(8), 774–785.

Chang, H. S., Lee, S. C., & Ji, Y. G. (2016). Wearable device adoption model with TAM and TTF. *International Journal of Mobile Communications, 14*(5), 518–537.

Chauhan, S., & Jaiswal, M. (2017). A meta-analysis of e-health applications acceptance: Moderating impact of user types and e-health application types. *Journal of Enterprise Information Management, 30*(2), 295–319.

Chen, K., & Chan, A. H. S. (2014). Gerontechnology acceptance by elderly Hong Kong Chinese: a senior technology acceptance model (STAM). *Ergonomics, 57*(5), 635–652.

Chen, C.-F., & Chen, P.-C. (2011). Applying the TAM to travelers' usage intentions of GPS devices. *Expert Systems with Applications, 38*(5), 6217–6221.

Chen, J.-F., Chang, J.-F., Kao, C.-W., & Huang, Y.-M. (2016). Integrating ISSM into TAM to enhance digital library services: A case study of the Taiwan Digital Meta-Library. *The Electronic Library, 34*(1), 58–73.

Chen, H., Rong, W., Ma, X., Qu, Y., & Xiong, Z. (2017). An extended technology acceptance model for mobile social gaming service popularity analysis. *Mobile Information Systems, 2017*, 1–12.

Chen, T., Chen, J., Or, C., & Lo, F. (2022). Path analysis of the roles of age, self-efficacy, and TAM constructs in the acceptance of performing upper limb exercises through immersive virtual reality games. *International Journal of Industrial Ergonomics, 91*, 103360. https://doi.org/10.1016/j.ergon.2022.103360

Cheng, S.-I., Chen, S.-C., & Yen, D. C. (2015). Continuance intention of e-portfolio system: A confirmatory and multigroup invariance analysis of technology acceptance model. *Computer Standards & Interfaces, 42*, 17–23.

Cheung, E. Y. M., & Sachs, J. (2006). Test of the technology acceptance model for a web-based information system in a Hong Kong Chinese sample. *Psychological Reports, 99*, 691–703.

Chiu, C.-M., Lin, H.-Y., Sun, S.-Y., & Hsu, M.-H. (2009). Understanding customers' loyalty intentions towards online shopping: An integration of technology acceptance model and fairness theory. *Behaviour & Information Technology, 28*(4), 347–360.

Choi, J. (2022). Enablers and inhibitors of smart city service adoption: A dual-factor approach based on the technology acceptance model. *Telematics and Informatics, 75*, 101911. https://doi.org/10.1016/j.tele.2022.101911

Choi, G., & Chung, H. (2013). Applying the technology acceptance model to social networking sites (SNS): Impact of subjective norm and social capital on the acceptance of SNS. *International Journal of Human-Computer Interaction, 29*(10), 619–628.

Chuttur, M. (2009). Overview of the technology acceptance model: Origins, developments and future directions. Indiana University, USA. *Sprouts: Working Papers on Information Systems, 9*(37), 1–21. http://sprouts.aisnet.org/9-37

Djamasbi, S., Strong, D. M., & Dishaw, M. (2010). Affect and acceptance: Examining the effects of positive mood on the technology acceptance model. *Decision Support Systems, 48*(2), 383–394.

Dogruel, L., Joeckel, S., & Bowman, N. D. (2015). The use and acceptance of new media entertainment technology by elderly users: development of an expanded technology acceptance model. *Behaviour & Information Technology, 34*(11), 1052–1063.

Egea, J. M. O., & González, M. V. R. (2022). Explaining physicians' acceptance of EHCR systems: An extension of TAM with trust and risk factors. *Computers in Human Behavior, 27*(1), 319–332.

Ge, Y., Qi, H., & Qu, W. (2023). The factors impacting the use of navigation systems: A study based on the technology acceptance model. *Transportation Research Part F: Traffic Psychology and Behaviour, 93*, 106–117. https://doi.org/10.1016/j.trf.2023.01.005

Gefen, D., & Straub, D. W. (1997). Gender difference in the perception and use of e-mail: An extension to the technology acceptance model. *MIS Quarterly, 21*(4), 389–400.

Girish, V. G., Kim, M., Sharma, I., & Lee, C.-K. (2022). Examining the structural relationships among e-learning interactivity, uncertainty avoidance, and perceived risks of COVID-19: Applying extended technology acceptance model. *International Journal of Human–Computer Interaction, 38*, 742–752. https://doi.org/10.1080/10447318.2021.1970430

Granić, A., & Marangunić, N. (2019). Technology acceptance model in educational context: A systematic literature review. *British Journal of Educational Technology, 50*(5), 2572–2593. https://doi.org/10.1111/bjet.12864

Gu, D., Khan, S., Khan, I. U., & Khan, S. U. (2019). Understanding mobile tourism shopping in Pakistan: An integrating framework of innovation diffusion theory and technology acceptance model. *Mobile Information Systems, 2019*, 1–18.

Guest, W., Wild, F., Vovk, A., Lefrere, P., Klemke, R., Fominykh, M., & Kuula, T. (2018). Technology acceptance model for augmented reality and wearable technologies. *Journal of Universal Computer Science, 24*(2), 192–219.

Guner, H., & Acarturk, C. (2020). The use and acceptance of ICT by senior citizens: A comparison of technology acceptance model (TAM) for elderly and young adults. *Universal Access in the Information Society, 19*, 311–330.

Horton, R. P., Buck, T., Waterson, P. E., & Clegg, C. W. (2001). Explaining intranet use with the technology acceptance model. *Journal of Information Technology, 16*(4), 237–249.

Hrastinski, S. (2008). What is online learner participation? A literature review. *Computers and Education, 51*, 1755–1765.

Hsiao, C.-H., Tang, K.-Y., & Lin, C.-H. (2015). Exploring college students' intention to adopt e-textbooks: A modified technology acceptance model. *Libri, 65*(2), 119–128.

Hsu, C.-L., & Lu, H.-P. (2004). Why do people play on-line games? An extended TAM with social influences and flow experience. *Information & Management, 41*(7), 853–868.

Hu, P. J., Chau, P. Y. K., Sheng, O. R. L., & Tam, K. Y. (1999). Examining the technology acceptance model using physician acceptance of telemedicine technology. *Journal of Management Information Systems, 16*(2), 91–112.

Huang, J.-H., Lin, Y.-R., & Chuang, S.-T. (2007). Elucidating user behavior of mobile learning: A perspective of the extended technology acceptance model. *The Electronic Library, 25*(5), 585–598.

Ingham, J., Cadieux, J., & Berrada, A. M. (2015). e-Shopping acceptance: A qualitative and meta-analytic review. *Information & Management, 52*(2015), 44–60.

Jan, A. U., & Contreras, V. (2011). Technology acceptance model for the use of information technology in universities. *Computers in Human Behavior, 27*(2), 845–851.

Jin, C.-H. (2014). Adoption of e-book among college students: The perspective of an integrated TAM. *Computers in Human Behavior, 41*, 471–477.

Jongchul, O., & Sung-Joon, Y. (2014). Validation of haptic enabling technology acceptance model (HE-TAM): Integration of IDT and TAM. *Telematics and Informatics, 31*(4), 585–596.

Joo, J., & Sang, Y. (2013). Exploring Koreans' smartphone usage: An integrated model of the technology acceptance model and uses and gratifications theory. *Computers in Human Behavior, 29*(6), 2512–2518.

Kanak, A., & Sogukpinar, I. (2017). BioTAM: A technology acceptance model for biometric authentication systems. *IET Biometrics, 6*(6), 457–467.

Kashi, K., & Zheng, C. (2013). Extending technology acceptance model to the e-recruitment context in Iran. *International Journal of Selection and Assessment, 21*(1), 121–129.

Kim, S. (2012). Factors affecting the use of social software: TAM perspectives. *The Electronic Library, 30*(5), 690–706.

Kim, J., & Forsythe, S. (2008). Sensory enabling technology acceptance model (SE-TAM): A multiple-group structural model comparison. *Psychology & Marketing, 25*(9), 901–922.

Kim, S., & Garrison, G. (2009). Investigating mobile wireless technology adoption: An extension of the technology acceptance model. *Information Systems Frontiers, 11*(3), 323–333.

King, W. R., & He, J. (2006). A meta-analysis of the technology acceptance model. *Information & Management, 43*, 740–755.

Kitchenham, B. (2004). Procedures for performing systematic reviews. NICTA Technical Report

Kwee-Meier, S. T., Bützler, J. E., & Schlick, C. (2016). Development and validation of a technology acceptance model for safety- enhancing, wearable locating systems. *Behaviour & Information Technology, 35(5)*, 394–409.

Lai, V. S., & Li, H. (2005). Technology acceptance model for internet banking: An invariance analysis. *Information & Management, 42(2)*, 373–386.

Lederer, A. L., Maupin, D. J., Sena, M. P., & Zhuang, Y. (2000). The technology acceptance model and the World Wide Web. *Decision Support Systems, 29(3)*, 269–282.

Lee, M.-C. (2009). Factors influencing the adoption of internet banking: An integration of TAM and TPB with perceived risk and perceived benefit. *Electronic Commerce Research and Applications, 8(3)*, 130–141.

Lee, H.-H., & Chang, E. (2011). Consumer attitudes toward online mass customization: An application of extended technology acceptance model. *Journal of Computer-Mediated Communication, 16(2)*, 171–200.

Lee, C., & Wan, G. (2010). Including subjective norm and technology trust in the technology acceptance model: A case of e-ticketing in China. *The DATA BASE for Advances in Information Systems, 41(4)*, 40–51.

Lee, Y.-H., Hsieh, Y.-C., & Chen, Y.-H. (2013). An investigation of employees' use of e-learning systems: applying the technology acceptance model. *Behaviour & Information Technology, 32(2)*, 173–189.

Lee, J. H., Kim, J. H., & Choi, J. Y. (2019). The adoption of virtual reality devices: The technology acceptance model integrating enjoyment, social interaction, and strength of the social ties. *Telematics and Informatics, 39*, 37–48.

Legris, P., Ingham, J., & Collerette, P. (2003). Why do people use information technology? A critical review of the technology acceptance model. *Information & Management, 40*, 191–204.

Leso, B. H., & Cortimiglia, M. N. (2022). The influence of user involvement in information system adoption: An extension of TAM. *Cognition, Technology & Work, 24*, 215–231. https://doi.org/10.1007/s10111-021-00685-w

Li, X.-Z., Chen, C.-C., Kang, X., & Kang, J. (2022). Research on relevant dimensions of tourism experience of intangible cultural heritage lantern festival: Integrating generic learning outcomes with the technology acceptance model. *Frontiers in Psychology, 13*, 943277. https://doi.org/10.3389/fpsyg.2022.943277

Lin, C. A., & Kim, T. (2016). Predicting user response to sponsored advertising on social media via the technology acceptance model. *Computers in Human Behavior, 64*, 710–718.

Lin, P.-H., & Yeh, S.-C. (2019). How motion-control influences a VR-supported technology for mental rotation learning: From the perspectives of playfulness, gender difference and technology acceptance model. *International Journal of Human–Computer Interaction, 35(18)*, 1736–1746.

Lopez-Nicolas, C., Molina-Castillo, F. J., & Bouwman, H. (2008). An assessment of advanced mobile services acceptance: Contributions from TAM and diffusion theory models. *Information & Management, 45(6)*, 359–364.

Lu, Y., Zhou, T., & Wang, B. (2009). Exploring Chinese users' acceptance of instant messaging using the theory of planned behavior, the technology acceptance model, and the flow theory. *Computers in Human Behavior, 25(1)*, 29–39.

Makki, T. W., DeCook, J. R., Kadylak, T., & Lee, O. J. Y. (2018). The social value of snapchat: An exploration of affiliation motivation, the technology acceptance model, and relational maintenance in snapchat use. *International Journal of Human–Computer Interaction, 34(5)*, 410–420.

Marangunić, N., & Granić, A. (2015). Technology acceptance model: A literature review from 1986. to 2013. *Universal Access Information Society, 14*, 81–95. https://doi.org/10.1007/s10209-014-0348-1

McFarland, D. J., & Hamilton, D. (2006). Adding contextual specificity to the technology acceptance model. *Computers in Human Behavior, 22(3)*, 427–447.

Mir, S. A., & Padma, T. (2020). Integrated technology acceptance model for the evaluation of agricultural decision support systems. *Journal of Global Information Technology Management, 23*(2), 138–164.

Mohammadi, H. (2015). Investigating users' perspectives on e-learning: An integration of TAM and IS success model. *Computers in Human Behavior, 45*, 359–374.

Moon, J. W., & Kim, Y. G. (2001). Extending the TAM for a World-Wide-Web context. *Information & Management, 38*(4), 217–230.

Mortenson, M. J., & Vidgen, R. (2016). A computational literature review of the technology acceptance model. *International Journal of Information Management, 36*, 1248–1259.

Nayak, L. U. S., Priest, L., & White, A. P. (2010). An application of the technology acceptance model to the level of Internet usage by older adults. *Universal Access in the Information Society, 9*(4), 367–374.

Ooi, K.-B., & Tan, G. W.-H. (2016). Mobile technology acceptance model: An investigation using mobile users to explore smartphone credit card. *Expert Systems with Applications, 59*(15), 33–46.

Oyman, M., Bal, D., & Ozer, S. (2022). Extending the technology acceptance model to explain how perceived augmented reality affects consumers' perceptions. *Computers in Human Behavior, 128*, 107127., ISSN 0747-5632. https://doi.org/10.1016/j.chb.2021.107127

Pan, S., & Jordan-Marsh, M. (2010). Internet use intention and adoption among Chinese older adults: From the expanded technology acceptance model perspective. *Computers in Human Behavior, 26*(5), 1111–1119.

Papakostas, C., Troussas, C., Krouska, A., & Sgouropoulou, C. (2023). Exploring users' behavioral intention to adopt mobile augmented reality in education through an extended technology acceptance model. *International Journal of Human–Computer Interaction, 39*(6), 1294–1302. https://doi.org/10.1080/10447318.2022.2062551

Park, E., & Kim, K. J. (2013). User acceptance of long-term evolution (LTE) services An application of extended technology acceptance model. *Program: Electronic Library and Information Systems, 47*(2), 188–205.

Park, E., & Kim, K. J. (2014). An integrated adoption model of mobile cloud services: Exploration of key determinants and extension of technology acceptance model. *Telematics and Informatics, 31*(3), 376–385.

Park, E., & Kwon, S. J. (2016). The adoption of teaching assistant robots: A technology acceptance model approach. *Program-Electronic Library and Information Systems, 50*(4), 354–366.

Park, N., Roman, R., Lee, S., & Chung, J. E. (2009). User acceptance of a digital library system in developing countries: An application of the technology acceptance model. *International Journal of Information Management, 29*(3), 196–209.

Park, E., Baek, S., Ohm, J., & Chang, H. J. (2014). Determinants of player acceptance of mobile social network games: An application of extended technology acceptance model. *Telematics and Informatics, 31*(1), 3–15.

Park, E., Kim, H., & Ohm, J. Y. (2015). Understanding driver adoption of car navigation systems using the extended technology acceptance model. *Behaviour & Information Technology, 34*(7), 741–751.

Pikkarainen, T., Pikkarainen, K., Karjaluoto, H., & Pahnila, S. (2004). Consumer acceptance of online banking: An extension of the technology acceptance model. *Internet Research, 14*(3), 224–235.

Razmak, J., & Bélanger, C. (2018). Using the technology acceptance model to predict patient attitude toward personal health records in regional communities. *Information Technology & People, 31*(2), 306–326.

Ren, L., Yang, F., Gu, C., Sun, J., & Liu, Y. (2022). A study of factors influencing Chinese college students' intention of using metaverse technology for basketball learning: Extending the technology acceptance model. *Frontiers in Psychology, 13*, 1049972. https://doi.org/10.3389/fpsyg.2022.1049972

Rigopoulou, I. D., Chaniotakis, I. E., & Kehagias, J. D. (2017). An extended technology acceptance model for predicting smartphone adoption among young consumers in Greece. *International Journal of Mobile Communications, 15*(4), 372–387.

Roberts, P., & Henderson, R. (2000). Information technology acceptance in a sample of government employees: A test of the technology acceptance model. *Interacting with Computers, 12*(5), 427–443.

Saade, R., & Bahli, B. (2005). The impact of cognitive absorption on perceived usefulness and perceived ease of use in on-line learning: An extension of the technology acceptance model. *Information & Management, 42*(2), 317–327.

Sagheer, N., Khan, K. I., Fahd, S., Mahmood, S., Rashid, T., & Jamil, H. (2022). Factors affecting adaptability of cryptocurrency: An application of technology acceptance model. *Frontiers in Psychology, 13*, 903473. https://doi.org/10.3389/fpsyg.2022.903473

Sagnier, C., Loup-Escande, E., Lourdeaux, D., Thouvenin, I., & Valléry, G. (2020). User acceptance of virtual reality: An extended technology acceptance model. *International Journal of Human-Computer Interaction, 36*(11), 1–15.

Sánchez, R. A., & Hueros, A. D. (2010). Motivational factors that influence the acceptance of Moodle using TAM. *Computers in Human Behavior, 26*(6), 1632–1640.

Sanchez-Prieto, J. C., Olmos-Miguelanez, S., & García-Penalvo, F. J. (2017). MLearning and pre-service teachers: An assessment of the behavioral intention using an expanded TAM model. *Computers in Human Behavior, 72*, 1–11.

Santini, F. O., Ladeira, W. J., Sampaio, C. H., Perin, M. G., & Dolci, P. C. (2019). Propensity for technological adoption: An analysis of effects size in the banking sector. *Behaviour & Information Technology, 38*(9), 1–15.

Schepers, J., & Wetzels, M. (2007). A meta-analysis of the technology acceptance model: Investigating subjective norm and moderation effects. *Information & Management, 44*, 90–103.

Scherer, R., Siddiq, F., & Tondeur, J. (2019). The technology acceptance model (TAM): A meta-analytic structural equation modeling approach to explaining teachers' adoption of digital technology in education. *Computers & Education, 128*, 13–35.

Sharma, S. K. (2019). Integrating cognitive antecedents into TAM to explain mobile banking behavioral intention: A SEM-neural network modelling. *Information Systems Frontiers, 21*, 815–827.

Sheikhshoaei, F., & Oloumi, T. (2011). Applying the technology acceptance model to Iranian engineering faculty libraries. *The Electronic Library, 29*(3), 367–378.

Shih, H. (2004). Extended technology acceptance model of internet utilization behavior. *Information & Management, 41*(6), 719–729.

Shin, D. H. (2009). Understanding user acceptance of DMB in South Korea using the modified technology acceptance model. *International Journal of Human-Computer Interaction, 25*(3), 173–198.

Shin, D.-H., & Kim, W.-Y. (2008). Applying the technology acceptance model and flow theory to cyworld user behavior: Implication of the web2.0 user acceptance. *Cyberpsychology & Behavior, 11*(3), 378–382.

Shyu, S. H.-P., & Huang, J.-H. (2011). Elucidating usage of e-government learning: A perspective of the extended technology acceptance model. *Government Information Quarterly, 28*(4), 491–502.

Siddaway, A. P., Wood, A. M., & Hedges, L. V. (2019). How to do a systematic review: Best practice guide for conducting and reporting narrative reviews, meta-analyses, and meta-syntheses. *Annual Review of Psychology, 70*, 747–770.

Sipior, J. C., Ward, B. T., & Connolly, R. (2011). The digital divide and t-government in the United States: Using the technology acceptance model to understand usage. *European Journal of Information Systems, 20*(3), 308–328.

Spacey, R., Goulding, A., & Murray, I. (2004). Exploring the attitudes of public library staff to the Internet using the TAM. *Journal of Documentation, 60*(5), 550–564.

Stern, B. B., Royne, M. B., Stafford, T. F., & Bienstock, C. C. (2008). Consumer acceptance of online auctions: An extension and revision of the TAM. *Psychology & Marketing, 25*(7), 619–636.

Šumak, B., Heričko, M., & Pušnik, M. (2011). A meta-analysis of e-learning technology acceptance: The role of user types and e-learning technology types. *Computers in Human Behavior, 27,* 2067–2077.

Šumak, B., Heričko, M., Budimac, Z., & Pušnik, M. (2017). Investigation of moderator factors in e-business adoption: A quantitative meta-analysis of moderating effects on the drivers of intention and behavior. *Computer Science and Information Systems, 14*(1), 75–102.

Svendsen, G. B., Johnsen, J.-A. K., Almås-Sørensen, L., & Vittersø, J. (2013). Personality and technology acceptance: The influence of personality factors on the core constructs of the technology acceptance model. *Behaviour & Information Technology, 32*(4), 323–334.

Tao, D., Wang, T., Wang, T., Zhang, T., Zhang, X., & Qu, X. (2020). A systematic review and meta-analysis of user acceptance of consumer-oriented health information technologies. *Computers in Human Behavior, 104,* 1–45.

Tavakoli, S. S., Mozaffari, A., Danaei, A., & Rashidi, E. (2023). Explaining the effect of artificial intelligence on the technology acceptance model in media: A cloud computing approach. *The Electronic Library, 41*(1), 1–29. https://doi.org/10.1108/EL-04-2022-0094

Tung, F.-C., Lee, M. S., Chen, C.-C., & Hsu, Y.-S. (2009). An extension of financial cost and TAM model with IDT for exploring users' behavioral intentions to use the CRM information system. *Social Behavior and Personality, 37*(5), 621–626.

Turner, M., Kitchenham, B., Brereton, P., Charters, S., & Budgen, D. (2010). Does the technology acceptance model predict actual use? A systematic literature review. *Information and Software Technology, 52,* 463–479.

Tzou, R.-C., & Lu, H.-P. (2009). Exploring the emotional, aesthetic, and ergonomic facets of innovative product on fashion technology acceptance model. *Behaviour & Information Technology, 28*(4), 311–322.

Verma, S., Bhattacharyya, S. S., & Kumar, S. (2018). An extension of the technology acceptance model in the big data analytics system implementation environment. *Information Processing & Management, 54*(5), 791–806.

Vijayasarathy, L. R. (2004). Predicting consumer intentions to use on-line shopping: The case for an augmented technology acceptance model. *Information & Management, 41*(6), 747–762.

Walldén, S., Makinen, E., & Raisamo, R. (2016). A review on objective measurement of usage in technology acceptance studies. *Universal Access in the Information Society, 15,* 713–726.

Wang, X., & Goh, D. H. (2017). Video game acceptance: A meta-analysis of the extended technology acceptance model. *Cyberpsychology, Behavior, and Social Networking, 20*(11), 662–671.

Wang, C., Cui, W., Zhang, Y., & Shen, H. (2022a). Exploring short video apps users' travel behavior intention: Empirical analysis based on SVA-TAM model. *Frontiers in Psychology, 13,* 912177. https://doi.org/10.3389/fpsyg.2022.912177

Wang, Y., Zhang, X., & Wang, L. (2022b). Assessing the intention to use sports bracelets among Chinese University Students: An extension of technology acceptance model with sports motivation. *Frontiers in Psychology, 13,* 846594. https://doi.org/10.3389/fpsyg.2022.846594

Webster, J., & Watson, R. T. (2002). Analyzing the past to prepare for the future: Writing a literature review. *MIS Quarterly, 26*(2), xiii–xxiii.

Wu, I.-L., & Chen, J.-L. (2005). An extension of Trust and TAM model with TPB in the initial adoption of on-line tax: An empirical study. *International Journal of Human-Computer Studies, 62*(6), 784–808.

Wu, B., & Chen, X. (2017). Continuance intention to use MOOCs: Integrating the technology acceptance model (TAM) and task technology fit (TTF) model. *Computers in Human Behavior, 67,* 1–12.

Wu, J., & Du, H. (2012). Toward a better understanding of behavioural intention and system usage constructs. *European Journal of Information Systems, 21,* 680–698.

Wu, J., & Lederer, A. (2009). A meta-analysis of the role of environment-based voluntariness in information technology acceptance. *MIS Quarterly, 33*(2), A-1–A-9.

Wu, J.-H., & Wang, S.-C. (2005). What drives mobile commerce? An empirical evaluation of the revised technology acceptance model. *Information & Management, 42*(5), 719–729.

Wu, K., Zhao, Y., Zhu, Q., Tan, X., & Zheng, H. (2011). A meta-analysis of the impact of trust on technology acceptance model: Investigation of moderating influence of subject and context type. *International Journal of Information Management, 31*(6), 572–581.

Xie, Q., Song, W., & Peng, X. (2017). Predictors for e-government adoption: Integrating TAM, TPB, trust and perceived risk. *The Electronic Library, 1*, 2–20.

Xu, N., Wang, K. J., & Lin, C. Y. (2022). Technology acceptance model for lawyer robots with AI: A quantitative survey. *International Journal of Social Robotics, 14*, 1043–1055. https://doi.org/10.1007/s12369-021-00850-1

Yang, H., & Yoo, Y. (2004). It's all about attitude: Revisiting the technology acceptance model. *Decision Support Systems, 38*(1), 19–31.

Yang, L., Bian, Y., Zhao, X., Liu, X., & Yao, X. (2021). Drivers' acceptance of mobile navigation applications: An extended technology acceptance model considering drivers' sense of direction, navigation application affinity and distraction perception. *International Journal of Human-Computer Studies, 145*, 102507. https://doi.org/10.1016/j.ijhcs.2020.102507

Yi, M. Y., & Hwang, Y. (2004). Predicting the use of web-based information systems: Self-efficacy, enjoyment, learning goal orientation, and the technology acceptance model. *International Journal of Human-Computer Studies, 59*(4), 431–449.

Yoon, H.-Y. (2016). User acceptance of mobile library applications in academic libraries: An application of the technology acceptance model. *The Journal of Academic Librarianship, 42*(6), 687–693.

Yoon, C. (2018). Extending the TAM for Green IT: A normative perspective. *Computers in Human Behavior, 83*, 129–139.

Yoon, C., & Kim, S. (2007). Convenience and TAM in a ubiquitous computing environment: The case of wireless LAN. *Electronic Commerce Research and Applications, 6*(1), 102–112.

Yousafzai, S. Y., Foxall, G. R., & Pallister, J. G. (2010). Explaining internet banking behavior: Theory of reasoned action, theory of planned behavior, or technology acceptance model? *Journal of Applied Social Psychology, 40*(5), 1172–1202.

Yu, Z. (2020). Visualizing co-citations of technology acceptance models in education. *Journal of Information Technology Research, 13*(1), 77–95.

Yu, X. (2022). Farmers' trust in government and participation intention toward rural tourism through TAM: The moderation effect of perceived risk. *Frontiers in Psychology, 13*, 1023280. https://doi.org/10.3389/fpsyg.2022.1023280

Yu, K., & Huang, G. (2020). Exploring consumers' intent to use smart libraries with technology acceptance model. *The Electronic Library, 38*(3), 447–461.

Yu, J., Ha, I., Choi, M., & Rho, J. (2005). Extending the TAM for a t-commerce. *Information & Management, 42*(7), 965–976.

Zainab, B., Awais Bhatti, M., & Alshagawi, M. (2017). Factors affecting e-training adoption: An examination of perceived cost, computer self-efficacy and the technology acceptance model. *Behaviour & Information Technology, 36*(12), 1261–1273.

Zobeidi, T., Homayoon, S. B., Yazdanpanah, M., Komendantova, N., & Warner, L. A. (2023). Employing the TAM in predicting the use of online learning during and beyond the COVID-19 pandemic. *Frontiers in Psychology, 14*, 1104653. https://doi.org/10.3389/fpsyg.2023.1104653

Chapter 4
Epilogue: What Will the Future of TAM Be Like?

Abstract The chapter explores the trajectory of the Technology Acceptance Model (TAM), characterized by its societal influence, capacity to handle and adapt to emerging challenges and commitment to ensuring that technology authentically serves and benefits the broader community. Through an analysis of TAM's historical development, current trends and potential future directions, it becomes evident that its future is dynamic. The chapter presents anticipated developments, including the integration of neuroscience perspectives, broader interdisciplinary collaboration, embracement of advanced methodologies, consideration of specific contextual intricacies, adoption of longitudinal and dynamic perspectives and a persistent commitment to ethical considerations. TAM is poised to remain a credible practical tool for predicting and explaining user acceptance. Its flexibility in addressing emerging complexities positions TAM at the forefront of comprehending and predicting user behaviours in the ever-changing landscape of technology acceptance and adoption. As we stand at the brink of a new technological era, the future of TAM presents both challenges and opportunities, urging examination to ensure innovative technologies align with user needs and preferences, facilitating their effective and seamless integration into various societal contexts.

Keywords Technology Acceptance Model · TAM · Dynamic future · Neuroscience perspectives · Societal influence

4.1 Societal Impact of TAM Research

Reflecting on three decades of the Technology Acceptance Model (TAM), it is crucial to project its course into the future and contemplate the potential societal impacts of TAM research. The model has not only shaped our understanding of technology adoption but has also influenced the design and implementation of various technological innovations across industries. Regardless of how promising, powerful or sophisticated a technology solution is, its ability to deliver benefits to society or industry depends on its acceptance and use by the target user population.

F. D. Davis, A. Granić, *The Technology Acceptance Model*, Human–Computer Interaction Series, https://doi.org/10.1007/978-3-030-45274-2_4

The fundamental premise of TAM underscores its critical role in ensuring that technological innovations align with user needs and preferences, contributing to their effective incorporation into diverse societal contexts.

The extensive scope of TAM's research and influence spans various domains, including learning, education, health, aging, government, community, sustainability, policy, economy, literacy, emergency response, medicine, the digital divide, human rights, disability, climate change, low-income populations, inequality, poverty and justice. This broad coverage reinforces TAM's relevance and impact across a variety of societal domains. Subsequently, we investigate a couple of domains to provide better insight, offering an illustration of the broad suitability of TAM.

Taking a closer look at the "health" category, studies have been published on a wide range of topics, illustrating the broad spectrum of technology acceptance within the healthcare sector. These studies delve into the acceptance of mobile health applications, electronic medical records (by physicians and staff), exergames, robotic health advisor, telemedicine, e-health portals, virtual reality for pain management, medical tourism, online health communities, weight management apps, knowledge-based clinical decision support, fitness apps, health care artificial intelligence, wearable sensors, robotic surgery, medical device implants etc. These studies collectively contribute to our understanding of technology acceptance in the healthcare domain.

Exploration of the "climate change" category reveals studies published on a fascinating diversity of topics, including the acceptance of smart grid technology, conservation agriculture, solar photovoltaics, mobile apps for recycling behaviour, decision support systems for water resource management, personal carbon footprint tracking and carbon-trading apps, smart thermostats and utility meters, electric vehicles, blockchains for foodservice supply chains, carbon capture and storage technologies, sustainable building construction, energy-efficient appliances, electric vehicles, ridesharing and additional examples. These studies enhance our comprehension of how technology is embraced in the context of climate change.

Upon investigating the societal impact of TAM research, it becomes evident that understanding user acceptance is crucial for realizing the intended benefits across society and industry. TAM's extensive influence, spanning healthcare, education, workplace, climate change and beyond, underscores its significance in shaping the technological landscape. This reflection on TAM's impact sets the stage for investigating future research directions. To unlock technology's full potential for societal advancement, it is imperative to address emerging issues and seize opportunities. The dynamic nature of technology, coupled with a continuous stream of new challenges, ensures ongoing opportunities for research and refinement. Therefore, the rest of the section delves into how TAM can be applied to specific contexts, including policy and governance, environmental sustainability and others. This analysis includes concrete examples and suggests potential research directions, providing a brief overview of TAM's applicability across various domains.

- *Education: adaptive learning platforms*
  In the realm of adaptive learning platforms, no matter how advanced the technology is in personalizing educational experiences, its effectiveness relies on the acceptance and engagement of students and educators. Research in this area should not only assess initial perceptions but also track the continuous usage patterns over time. Understanding the evolving dynamics of acceptance is essential for refining these platforms and ensuring they align with the educational goals and preferences of the users.
- *Policy and governance: e-government services*
  For e-government services to fulfil their potential in enhancing civic engagement and streamlining governance, they must be embraced by the citizens. Policymakers need to pay attention to factors influencing acceptance, such as trust, ease of use and perceived utility. Ongoing research should delve into the evolving attitudes of users towards e-government platforms, recognizing that sustained use is crucial for harvesting the societal benefits of digitized government services.
- *Healthcare: telemedicine adoption*
  The rapid expansion of telemedicine during global challenges highlighted its potential, but for it to truly transform healthcare, it must be embraced by both patients and healthcare providers. Continued research is imperative to understand the factors influencing ongoing acceptance. Patient satisfaction, healthcare provider experiences, and the integration of telemedicine into broader healthcare systems require sustained investigation to ensure that the promised benefits of remote healthcare delivery are realized.
- *Environmental sustainability: acceptance of smart grid technologies*
  Smart grid technologies hold the promise of more sustainable and efficient energy management. However, their success is contingent on the acceptance and active participation of consumers. Research should focus not only on the initial perceptions of users but also on their ongoing engagement with smart grid technologies. This nuanced understanding is crucial for refining strategies that promote sustained acceptance, ultimately leading to more effective and sustainable energy practices.
- *Workplace innovation: acceptance of remote work technologies*
  The shift to remote work technologies has reshaped the modern workplace, but their continued success depends on user acceptance. Research should go beyond the initial adoption phase and explore how remote work technologies impact employee productivity, collaboration and job satisfaction over time. This longitudinal perspective is vital for organizations and policymakers to adapt strategies that foster a positive and sustained relationship between users and technology.
- *Social inclusion: digital literacy programs*
  Digital literacy programs are designed to empower individuals, but their success relies on the ongoing engagement and acceptance of the target population. Research should not only evaluate the immediate outcomes of these programs but also track the long-term impact on participants' lives. Understanding how digital literacy contributes to social inclusion over time is essential for refining program designs and ensuring that the benefits reach marginalized communities.

Evidently, TAM stands as a pivotal framework, shaping our understanding of technology adoption and influencing the design and implementation of innovative solutions across diverse societal domains in the years to come. The continuous stream of challenges in the evolving technological landscape necessitates ongoing investigation and refinement, emphasizing the lasting relevance of TAM. In essence, TAM's journey from the past to the future is marked by its societal impact, flexibility in addressing emerging challenges and a commitment to ensuring that technology truly serves and benefits society at large.

4.2 NeuroIS Research Extending TAM

NeuroIS (Neuro Information Systems) refers to the interdisciplinary field studying the intersection of neuroscience and information systems (IS). It involves the application of neurophysiological tools, as well as the utilization of theories and concepts from neuroscience to deepen our understanding of the neural processes underlying technology acceptance, going beyond traditional behavioural measures (Riedl et al., 2020).

Fred Davis has played a key role in establishing NeuroIS as a recognized and influential field within the broader realm of IS. He became interested in using cognitive neuroscience methods for IS research in the early 2000s. It had become increasingly difficult to make theoretical advances in research on the Technology Acceptance Model (TAM) using traditional methods like self-report measures, surveys and behavioural experiments. While TAM research had established a core model and many useful extensions ("TAM++"), substantial unexplained variance in user behaviour remained. Meanwhile, advances in neuroimaging were enabling interesting research on human behaviour in neuroeconomics and social cognitive neuroscience.

Cognitive neuroscience offered the opportunity to "open up the black box" of the brain to gain deeper insights into the neural processes underlying users' moment-to-moment cognitive, emotional and perceptual/attentional processes. Many neural processes are unconscious and too rapid or fleeting to be captured with traditional methods. Overall, cognitive neuroscience has the potential "to substantially expand the domain of applicability for TAM theories beyond controlled conscious processes to encompass the fundamental role of automatic unconscious processes" (Dimoka et al., 2007, p. 9).

It has now been confirmed that NeuroIS Research routinely produces new insights that go beyond research based on traditional methods, often by examining constructs or phenomena that are difficult or impossible to capture with traditional methods. When research has used both traditional and NeuroIS methods to measure the same construct in a single study (e.g. emotion, cognitive load, perceptions etc.), it typically finds that traditional and NeuroIS measures are distinct, and each explains unique variance in key dependent variables like user behaviour or performance. Thus, NeuroIS has succeeded in advancing TAM++ and other IS research beyond what was possible to observe via traditional methods.

Exploring the concept of NeuroIS research extending the Technology Acceptance Model (TAM) unveils valuable insights for shaping the future trajectory of TAM. These insights underscore the ongoing evolution of TAM, boosted by the integration of neuroscience perspectives. Concrete examples illuminate the ways in which NeuroIS enhances TAM, contributing to tangible advancements. The envisioned future of TAM spans from the development of personalized models and ethical considerations to fostering cross-disciplinary collaboration and practical applications. This path signifies a sophisticated, adaptive and ethically conscious understanding of technology acceptance and adoption. Further explanation of these prospective advancements provides key observations to support this transformative journey.

– *Neuroscientific insights and TAM evolution*
  The integration of neuroscientific insights into TAM represents a significant advancement in understanding the neural processes underlying technology acceptance. Continued collaboration between IS researchers and neuroscientists can lead to a more refined or sophisticated version of TAM that incorporates real-time neurophysiological measures. This could involve techniques such as functional magnetic resonance imaging (fMRI) or electroencephalography (EEG) to capture brain activity during technology interactions, providing a deeper understanding of cognitive and emotional responses.
– *Personalization and individualization*
  TAM, in its conventional form, offers a broad framework for comprehending user acceptance. NeuroIS research has the potential to contribute to the creation of personalized TAM models, acknowledging that individual differences in neurobiology may impact technology acceptance uniquely. Tailored TAM frameworks, which take into account individual user profiles, considering factors such as cognitive styles, emotional responses and attentional processes, could provide more accurate predictions of technology adoption and use. For instance, a healthcare application utilizing neurophysiological data to customize its interface and features based on individual cognitive preferences and emotional responses could result in a more personalized and effective user experience.
– *Ethical considerations and responsible use*
  The integration of neuroscience into TAM raises ethical considerations related to privacy, consent and the responsible use of neurophysiological data. Future TAM research may delve deeper into ethical frameworks for NeuroIS, ensuring that the collection and analysis of neurophysiological data adhere to strict standards. This is crucial for maintaining user trust and addressing concerns related to the potential misuse of sensitive information. For example, a study could examine the implementation of neuroethical guidelines in the design of consumer-oriented brain-computer interface (BCI) devices, ensuring transparent data usage and robust privacy protection.
– *Cross-disciplinary collaboration*
  The collaboration between IS and neuroscience researchers has advanced NeuroIS, already expanding the interdisciplinary nature of TAM. The future of TAM may involve even broader cross-disciplinary collaborations, encompassing

experts from fields such as bioethics, psychology and data science. This holistic, cross-disciplinary approach could lead to a more comprehensive understanding of technology acceptance in diverse contexts. For instance, a study might bring together IS researchers, neuroscientists and psychologists to investigate the impact of cultural factors on the neurological markers linked to the acceptance of technology.

– *Longitudinal and dynamic perspectives*
  TAM's evolution will likely incorporate more longitudinal and dynamic perspectives to explore the evolution of user attitudes over time. The integration of neuroscience methods into longitudinal studies could offer insights into the neurobiological changes associated with prolonged technology use. Understanding how the brain adapts to and adopts technology over time can shape the future development of TAM. For example, a study tracking users' neurophysiological responses to a social media platform over several years could unveil neural adaptations, shedding light on the long-term effects of technology use and informing the evolution of TAM.

– *Practical applications and real-world impact*
  NeuroIS research has theoretical implications for understanding cognitive and affective aspects of technology acceptance. The future of TAM may involve a more direct translation of NeuroIS insights into practical applications, influencing the design of user interfaces, marketing strategies, educational interventions and workplace technologies leading to more usable and effective outcomes. Bridging the gap between theory and application, TAM is poised to have a more immediate impact on user experiences. For instance, a company could leverage neurophysiological insights to design workplace technologies that enhance employee satisfaction and productivity. This could be achieved by adapting interfaces based on real-time neural data, creating a more user-friendly work environment.

In summary, the future of TAM, shaped by the integration of NeuroIS research, promises greater personalization, heightened ethical considerations, cross-disciplinary collaboration, a focus on longitudinal perspectives and practical applications that enhance real-world impact. The synergy between TAM and neuroscience insights positions this model as a vital tool for understanding and predicting user behaviour in the evolving landscape of technology acceptance.

References

Dimoka, A., Pavlou, P., & Davis, F. D. (2007). *Neuro-IS: The potential of cognitive neuroscience for information systems research*. In Association for Information Systems (Ed.), Proceedings of the international conference on information systems, ICIS 2007 (pp. 1–22). http://aisel.aisnet.org/icis2007/122

Riedl, R., Fischer, T., Léger, P. M., & Davis, F. D. (2020). A decade of NeuroIS research. *The Database for Advances in Information Systems, 51*(3), 13–54. https://doi.org/10.1145/3410977.3410980

Chapter 5
Actionable Principles: The Seven Pillars Framework

Abstract The chapter introduces the Seven Pillars Framework, serving as a strategic guide for researchers and practitioners who aim to customize the TAM++ body of knowledge for application-oriented studies within specific contexts. Presented in a comprehensive table, this Framework outlines seven actionable principles with practical applications demonstrated through real-world examples. These principles function as effective guiding concepts, facilitating the achievement of specific goals in the exploration of technology acceptance across a wide array of technological solutions. Enriched with initial reference points and model names, the Framework holds significant promise for enhancing research and practice in the dynamic field of technology acceptance and adoption.

Keywords Actionable principles · The Seven Pillars Framework · Technology Acceptance Model · TAM

Within the Seven Pillars Framework outlined in the chapter, researchers and practitioners are provided guidance on customizing the TAM++ body of knowledge for their application-oriented studies within specific contexts. *The Seven Pillars Framework* presents seven actionable principles in a clear and concise manner, emphasizing that these principles not only serve as guiding concepts but are also practical and applicable in real-world situations to achieve specific goals. The Framework is detailed in Table 5.1, where each actionable principle is accompanied by a relevant explanation, a concrete example of an application-based study and a detailed account of how the particular principle is implemented and put into practice in that specific case. It is important to note that the provided examples and existing model names act as initial reference points. The selection of models, theories, constructs and variables should be contingent upon unique research goals, technology characteristics and the specific context in question.

F. D. Davis, A. Granić, *The Technology Acceptance Model*, Human–Computer Interaction Series, https://doi.org/10.1007/978-3-030-45274-2_5

Table 5.1 Actionable principles: The seven pillars framework

The seven pillars framework

Actionable Principle 1:
Use the core TAM, which includes generalized direct determinants of behavioural intention (BI), to establish a foundation and baseline; this helps guard against serious omitted variable biases.

● Explanation:
This principle recommends utilizing the core Technology Acceptance Model (TAM), which incorporates common direct determinants of behavioural intention (BI). By doing so, you establish a solid foundation and baseline for your study. Additionally, employing the core TAM helps mitigate the risk of serious omitted variable biases, ensuring a more accurate understanding of user behaviour towards technology adoption.

● Example: *Investigating Employee Acceptance of New Project Management Software*
Imagine you are conducting research to understand employees' acceptance of a new project management software within a company. The core determinants in the TAM model, which includes perceived usefulness and perceived ease of use, are crucial in predicting behavioural intention to adopt the technology.

● In applying the actionable principle:
Establishing a Foundation and Baseline: You decide to use the core TAM as the basis for your study. You carefully measure and analyse perceived usefulness and perceived ease of use as they relate to employees' behavioural intention to adopt the new project management software.
Mitigating Omitted Variable Biases: Let us say you identify additional factors that could influence technology acceptance, such as the level of technical support provided and the employees' prior experience with similar software. Instead of neglecting these factors, you incorporate them into your study, expanding the scope beyond the core TAM if necessary. By doing this, you guard against serious omitted variable biases. Without considering these additional factors, your study might have overlooked crucial elements that impact employees' behavioural intention.
Ensuring Accuracy: The use of the core TAM as a foundation ensures that you are not missing key determinants of behavioural intention. This, in turn, contributes to the accuracy of your findings and enhances the reliability of predictions regarding employees' acceptance of the new project management software.

(continued)

Table 5.1 (continued)

The seven pillars framework

Actionable Principle 2:

When faced with a prohibitively large number of antecedents to the core behavioural intention (BI) determinants, choose those that are likely to be active and relevant links in the causal chain connecting your interventions to core BI determinants.

- Explanation:

This principle advises researchers or practitioners to make strategic choices when dealing with a large number of potential antecedents (predictors) that could influence the core behavioural intention (BI) determinants. Instead of trying to address all possible antecedents, focus on selecting those that are most likely to be actively and directly linked in the causal chain, connecting your interventions to the core BI determinants.

- Example: *Understanding Customer Purchase Intentions in E-commerce*

Imagine you are working on improving customer purchase intentions in an e-commerce setting. The core BI determinants, in this case, might include factors such as perceived usefulness, perceived ease of use and trust in the online platform.

- In applying the actionable principle:

Prohibitively Large Number of Antecedents: As you explore the literature and conduct preliminary research, you discover a vast array of potential antecedents to customer purchase intentions. These may include factors like advertising effectiveness, website design, social media presence, customer reviews and more.

Choosing Active and Relevant Links: Faced with the challenge of addressing a multitude of potential antecedents, you strategically choose those that are likely to be active and relevant links in the causal chain. Instead of attempting to address all possible factors, you focus on, for example, advertising effectiveness, website design and customer reviews. These antecedents are chosen based on previous research indicating their strong influence on perceived usefulness, perceived ease of use and trust, which are core BI determinants.

Causal Chain to Core BI Determinants: Your hypothesis is that improvements in advertising effectiveness and website design directly impact perceived usefulness and perceived ease of use, while positive customer reviews directly influence trust in the online platform. In designing interventions to enhance customer purchase intentions, you concentrate resources on improving advertising strategies, optimizing website design and encouraging positive customer reviews. These interventions are chosen strategically based on their direct and relevant links to the core BI determinants.

Effectiveness Assessment: As you implement these interventions, you systematically assess their impact on the core BI determinants and, consequently, on customer purchase intentions. This focused approach allows for a more targeted evaluation of the effectiveness of your interventions.

(continued)

Table 5.1 (continued)

The seven pillars framework

Actionable Principle 3:
Consult context-specific meta-analyses to identify potentially relevant core behavioural intention (BI) antecedents.

- Explanation:

This principle advises consulting meta-analyses that are specific to the context in question. The goal is to identify potential antecedents (predictors) that are relevant to the core behavioural intention (BI) determinants in the specific context you are working in.

- Example: *Uncovering Factors Shaping Employee Adoption of New Tools*

Let us say you are working in the context of employee performance and want to understand the factors influencing employees' intention to adopt a new productivity tool. The core BI determinants in this case might include factors like perceived usefulness and perceived ease of use of the tool.

- In applying the actionable principle:

Context-Specific Meta-Analyses: You search for existing meta-analyses that have been conducted specifically in the context of workplace technology adoption or employee performance improvement. These meta-analyses aggregate findings from various studies related to your specific context.

Identify Potentially Relevant Core BI Antecedents: Through consulting these meta-analyses, you identify potential antecedents that have been consistently shown to be relevant in similar workplace contexts. For instance, you find that factors like perceived organizational support, training effectiveness and supervisor encouragement have consistently been identified as relevant antecedents in similar studies. Equipped with this information, you incorporate these identified antecedents into your study. For example, you might design interventions that focus not only on the perceived usefulness of the new productivity tool but also on improving organizational support and providing effective training.

(continued)

Table 5.1 (continued)

The seven pillars framework

Actionable Principle 4:
Moderators are good for tailoring the theory to specific contexts, but beware of too many moderators that add to the complexity, reduce the interpretability and comprehensibility of results.

- Explanation:

This principle suggests that while moderators (variables that influence the strength or direction of a relationship between two other variables) can be beneficial for customizing a theory to specific contexts, caution should be exercised to avoid an excessive number of moderators. Too many moderators can introduce unnecessary complexity, making it challenging to interpret and comprehend the study results effectively.

- Example: *Age and Online Shopping: Unveiling Influencing Factors*

Consider a study investigating the factors influencing online shopping behaviour among different age groups. The core theory includes variables like perceived ease of use, perceived usefulness and trust as determinants of online shopping intentions. You want to tailor the theory to specific age groups (young adults, middle-aged, and seniors) using moderators.

- In applying the actionable principle:

Tailoring the Theory with Moderators: Recognizing that age may influence the relationships between the core variables, you introduce age as a moderator. For example, you hypothesize that the impact of trust on online shopping intentions may vary across age groups.

Beware of Too Many Moderators: While age is a relevant moderator, you need to be cautious not to introduce too many additional moderators, such as income, education level and technological expertise. Each additional moderator adds complexity to the study. If you include numerous moderators, the model becomes complicated, and interpreting the interplay between variables becomes challenging. The study may become less comprehensible to both researchers and readers.

Impact on Interpretability and Comprehensibility: For instance, if you introduce age, income, education level and technological expertise as moderators simultaneously, the results may become difficult to interpret. It may be unclear whether observed effects are due to the core variables or interactions with the numerous moderators. This complexity can reduce the comprehensibility of the study results, potentially limiting the practical insights that can be drawn.

(continued)

Table 5.1 (continued)

The seven pillars framework

Actionable Principle 5:
Consider opportunities to integrate well-established theories from sister disciplines.
- Explanation:
This principle encourages researchers or practitioners to explore the potential benefits of incorporating well-established theories from related or "sister" disciplines into their work, thereby spanning diverse multidisciplinary domains. Doing so can enhance the robustness, depth and applicability of the study.
- Example: *Exploring Pro-environmental Behaviour in Environmental Psychology Research*
Suppose you are conducting research in the field of environmental psychology to understand individuals' pro-environmental behaviour, specifically their willingness to adopt sustainable practices in the workplace.
- In applying the actionable principle:
Core Theory in Environmental Psychology: The core theory in environmental psychology might involve variables such as environmental awareness, personal values, and perceived behavioural control, all influencing pro-environmental behaviour.
Opportunity for Integration: Recognizing the interdisciplinary nature of environmental issues, you consider integrating well-established theories from sister disciplines, such as behavioural economics and social psychology.
Integration of Prospect Theory (Behavioural Economics): You decide to integrate Prospect Theory from behavioural economics, which explains how individuals make decisions under uncertainty. This theory suggests that individuals may be more motivated to adopt sustainable practices if they perceive the potential gains (e.g. cost savings) as outweighing the losses.
Integration of Social Identity Theory (Social Psychology): Additionally, you integrate Social Identity Theory from social psychology, which highlights the role of group identities in shaping behaviour. In this context, individuals may be more inclined to adopt pro-environmental behaviours if they identify with a workplace culture that values sustainability.
Benefits of Integration: The integration of these theories enriches your study by providing a more comprehensive understanding of the factors influencing pro-environmental behaviour. You go beyond the traditional environmental psychology framework to consider cognitive decision-making processes (Prospect Theory) and social dynamics (Social Identity Theory).The integrated (hybrid) approach not only contributes to theoretical advancement but also has practical implications. For example, interventions aimed at promoting sustainable behaviours in the workplace may be designed with insights from both environmental psychology and the integrated theories.

(continued)

Table 5.1   (continued)

The seven pillars framework

Actionable Principle 6:
Where possible, consider a strategy of comparing competing models and then synthesizing/integrating the best parts of the competing models to form a new model.
- Explanation:
This principle suggests a strategic approach when faced with multiple competing models in a given field. Instead of adopting a single existing model, consider comparing and contrasting different models and then synthesizing or integrating the most effective constructs to create a new, more robust model.
- Example: *Analysing Student Academic Performance*
Suppose you are conducting research to understand the factors influencing student academic performance. In the literature, you come across two competing models: the Socioeconomic Status (SES) Model and the Self-Determination Theory (SDT).
- In applying the actionable principle:
Competing Models: The SES Model emphasizes the role of socioeconomic factors, such as parental education, income and family background, in influencing academic performance. The SDT suggests that intrinsic motivation, autonomy and relatedness are critical factors influencing student engagement and academic success.
Strategy of Comparing Models: Instead of adopting one model exclusively, you decide to compare the two models. You review empirical studies and assess how well each model explains variations in student academic performance across diverse student populations. Through your analysis, you find that the SES Model provides valuable insights into the impact of socioeconomic factors on academic performance, while the SDT highlights the importance of intrinsic motivation and psychological needs.
Forming a New Integrated (Hybrid) Model: Drawing on the strengths of both models, you synthesize an integrated model that incorporates socioeconomic factors from the SES Model and motivational factors from the SDT. This new model aims to capture the multidimensional nature of student academic performance and provides a more refined comprehension of academic performance by considering both external factors (socioeconomic) and internal factors (motivation).
Validation and Application: You validate the integrated (hybrid) model through a comprehensive study involving diverse student populations. The results show that the integrated model offers better predictive power and explanatory capacity compared to using either the SES Model or SDT in isolation.

(continued)

Table 5.1 (continued)

The seven pillars framework

Actionable Principle 7:
Carefully balance the trade-off between simplicity/parsimony and richness/complexity.
- Explanation:
This principle advises researchers to strike a careful balance when developing models or theories. On one hand, simplicity, or parsimony, involves creating a model with the fewest variables necessary to explain a phenomenon. On the other hand, richness, or complexity, involves incorporating additional variables to capture the multifaceted nature of the phenomenon. Balancing this trade-off is crucial to avoid oversimplification or excessive complexity, ensuring that the model is both manageable and insightful.
- Example: *Developing a Model for Employee Job Satisfaction*
Suppose you are a researcher studying factors influencing employee job satisfaction. The actionable principle of balancing simplicity and richness is applied as follows.
- In applying the actionable principle:
Simplicity/Parsimony: You recognize the importance of simplicity to create a model that is easy to understand, communicate and analyse. You start with a core set of variables — workload, interpersonal relationships, and compensation — acknowledging that these are well-established factors influencing job satisfaction.
Richness/Complexity: However, you also acknowledge the need for richness to capture the complexity of job satisfaction. You are aware that employee satisfaction is influenced by various psychological, organizational and contextual factors.
Balancing the Trade-off: To achieve balance, you carefully evaluate the necessity of each variable. You consider the theoretical and empirical support for each factor and its practical relevance to the specific organizational context. After thorough consideration, you decide to include workload, interpersonal relationships and compensation as core variables. Additionally, you add organizational support, recognizing its significance in the organizational context under study. By adding organizational support, you introduce richness without overwhelming the model. Organizational support is chosen strategically, considering its theoretical importance and relevance to the study objectives.
Advantages of the Balanced Model: The balanced model includes enough variables to provide a thorough understanding of employee job satisfaction. It is neither overly simplistic nor excessively complex, ensuring that it remains manageable for analysis and interpretation. Such model facilitates practical application and communication. Stakeholders can grasp the essential factors influencing job satisfaction without being overwhelmed by unnecessary complexity. The model retains sufficient richness to inform organizational strategies and interventions effectively.

While formulating the principles, due acknowledgment is given to the relevant body of research, with special recognition of the guidelines by Hong et al. (2014) for developing context-specific models, the recommendations for future UTAUT-based research on technology acceptance and use presented by Venkatesh et al. (2016) as well as the systematic approach referred to as Technology Acceptance and Adoption Research Approach (TA2RA), introduced by Granić (2024). The Seven Pillars Framework has significant potential to offer benefits to researchers and practitioners in the field of technology acceptance as they conduct their own studies. This is attributed to a few key reasons outlined below, as the Framework:

- Directs researchers to commence with the core TAM as a robust starting point, ensuring a comprehensive understanding of technology adoption by considering key determinants
- Leads researchers to be strategic in their selection of antecedents when faced with a large number of potential influences on core behavioural intention determinants
- Guides researchers to leverage existing context-specific meta-analyses to inform their understanding of potentially influential antecedents
- Advises researchers to carefully balance the use of moderators to tailor a theory to specific contexts
- Encourages researchers to look beyond the boundaries of their specific discipline and consider incorporating well-established theories from related disciplines
- Suggests researchers to combine the best aspects of different models to create a stronger, more effective model when faced with multiple options in a field
- Directs researchers to balance simplicity and richness in order to create models that are both manageable and comprehensive

In conclusion, those who adopt the Seven Pillars Framework gain a strategic tool to navigate the intricacies of technology acceptance. This allows them to tailor their research to specific contexts and allocate their intellectual efforts efficiently for maximum impact.

References

Granić, A. (2024). User acceptance of interactive technologies. In C. Stephanidis & G. Salvendy (Eds.), *Foundations and fundamentals in human-computer interaction (Volume I)* (Handbook of human-computer interaction: Foundations and advances, 6-Volume set, 1st Edition). ISBN 9781032750842. CRC Press, Taylor & Francis Group, LLC.

Hong, W., Chan, F. K. Y., Thong, J. Y. L., Chasalow, L. C., & Dhillon, G. (2014). A framework and guidelines for context-specific theorizing in information systems research. *Information System Research, 25*(1), 111–136. https://www.jstor.org/stable/24700108.

Venkatesh, V., Thong, J. Y. L., & Xu, X. (2016). Unified theory of acceptance and use of technology: a synthesis and the road ahead. *Journal of the Association for Information Systems, 17*(5), 328–376. https://doi.org/10.17705/1jais.00428

Printed in the United States
by Baker & Taylor Publisher Services